I0468780

Calmtangles
Adult Coloring Book

Over 50 Zentangles to Color
One image per page

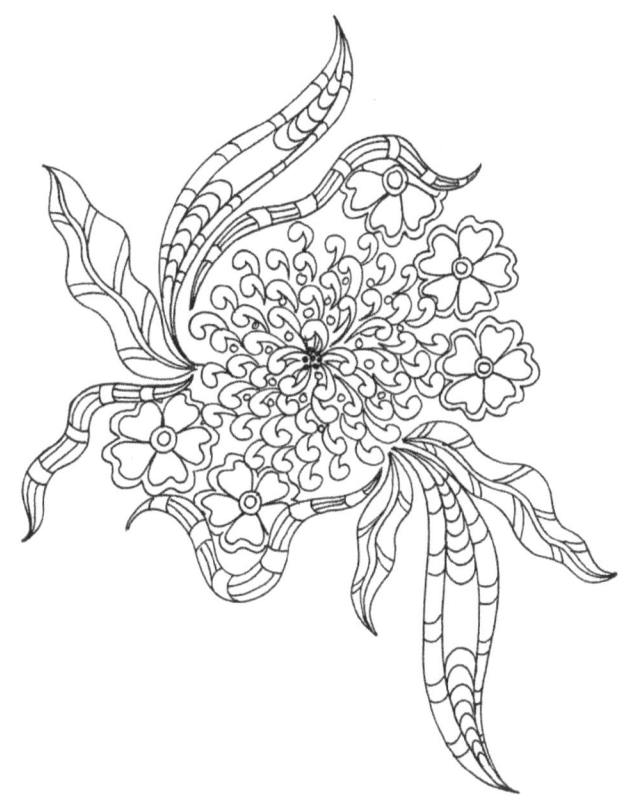

Go to: www.calmdalas.com

Get 10 **FREE** Zentangles and be notified about new books!

Copyright © 2016 Doyle

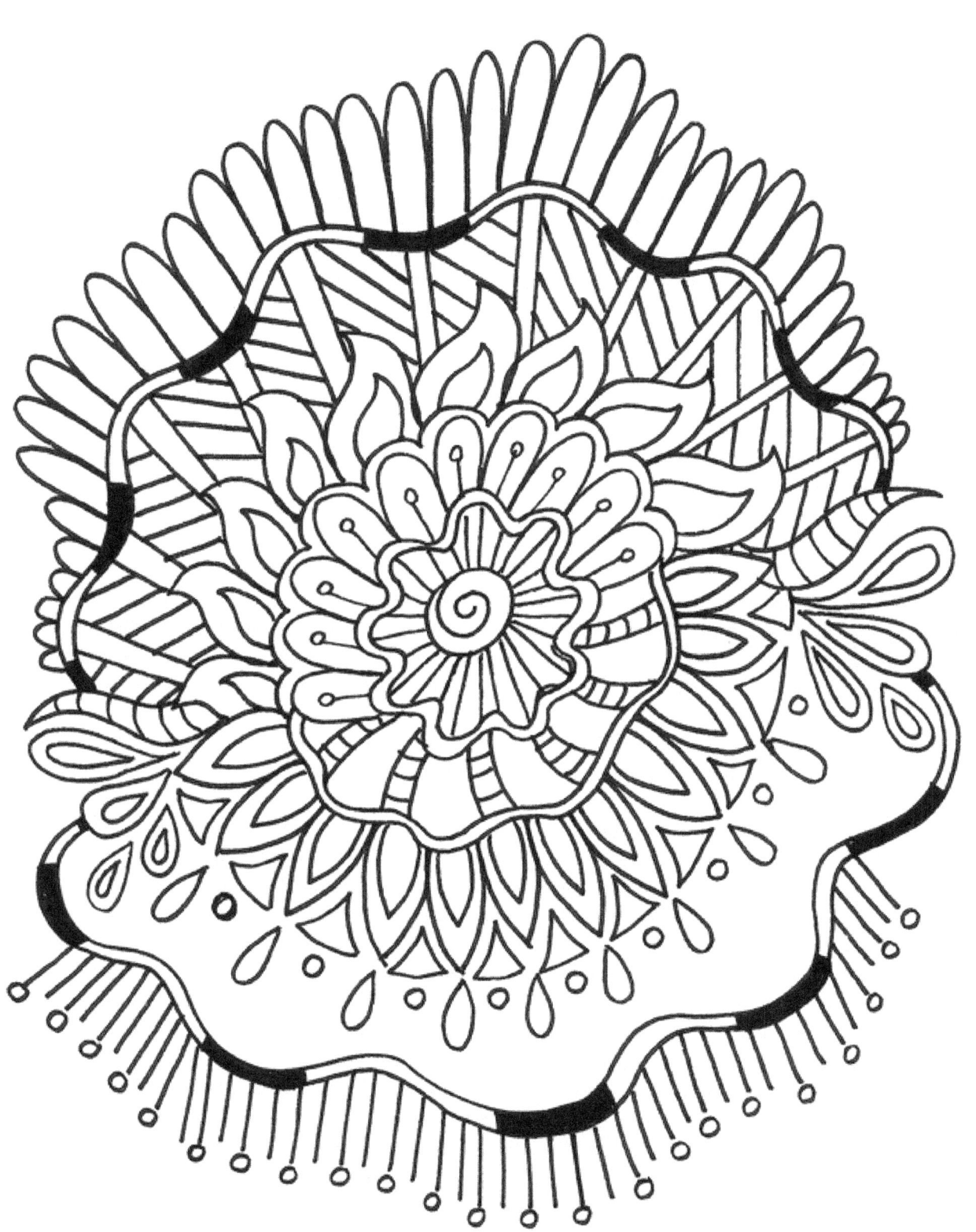

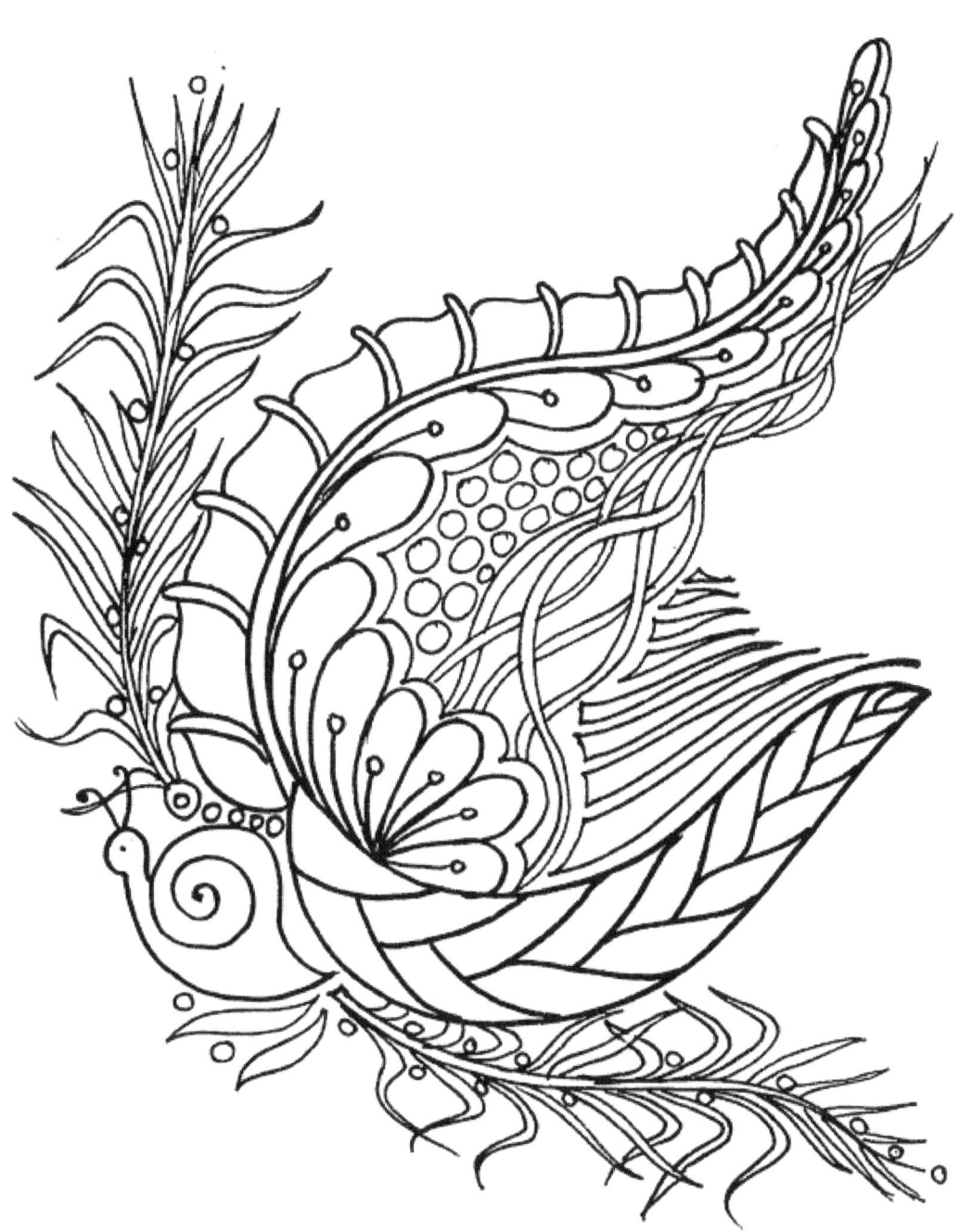

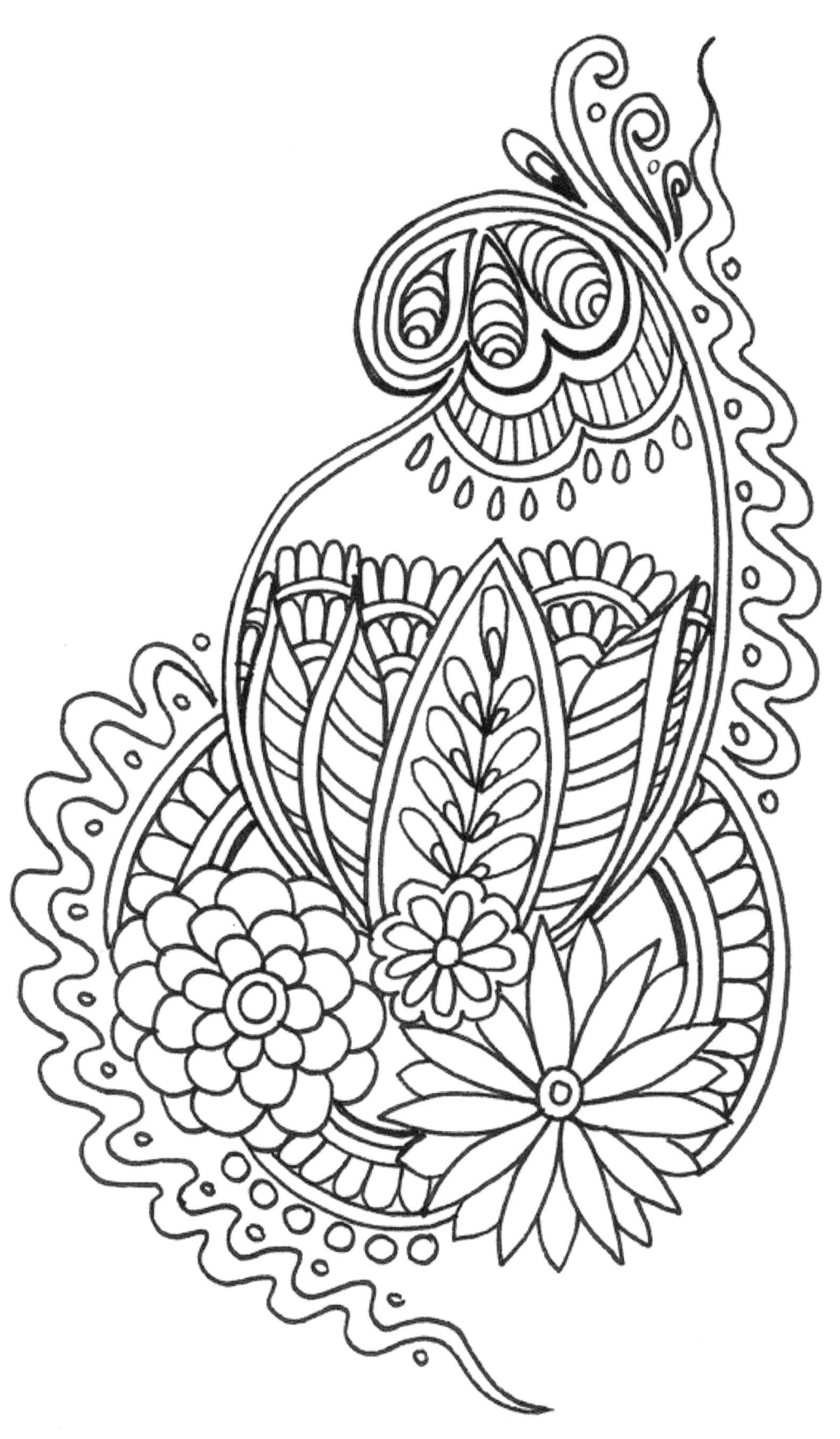

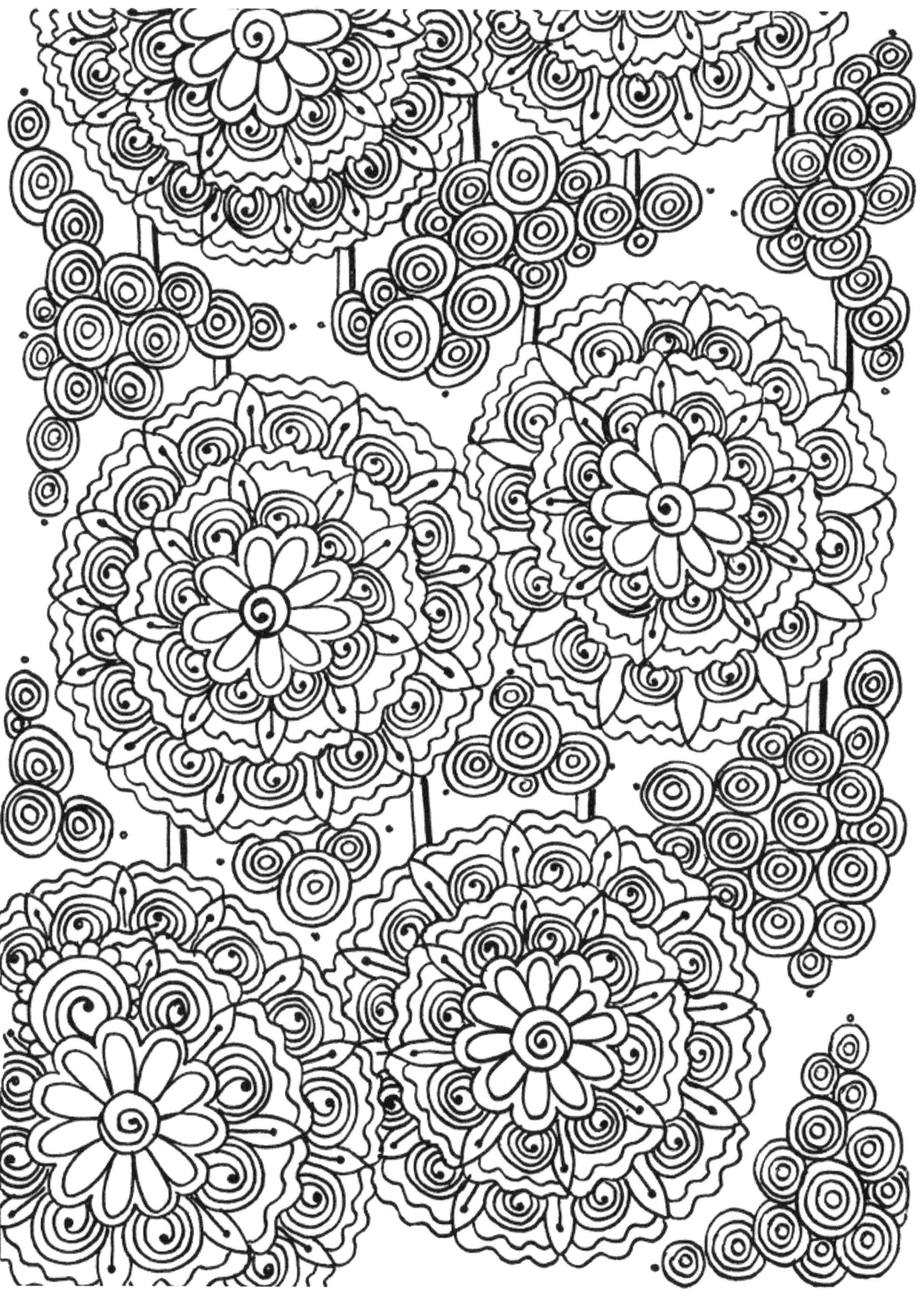

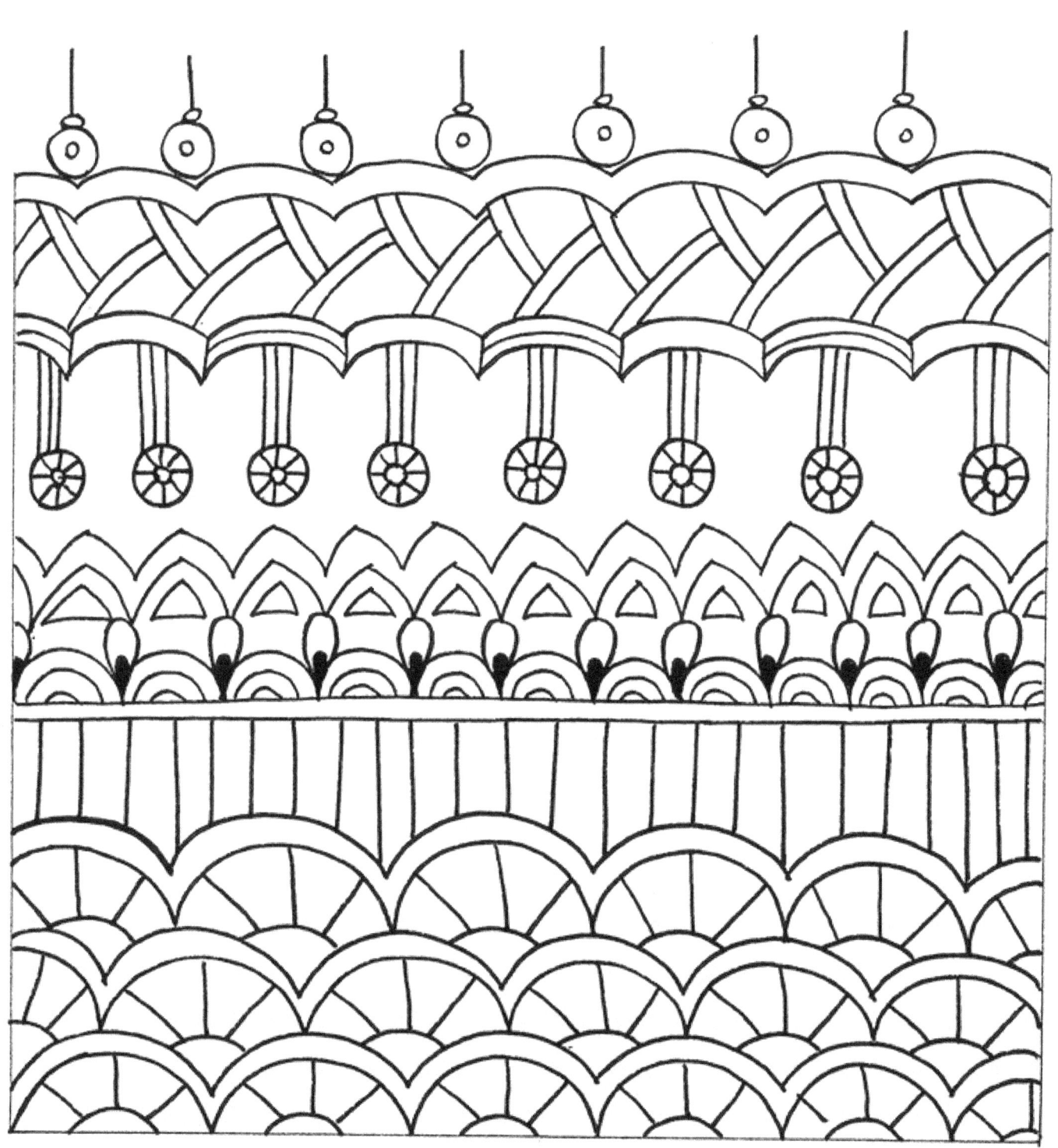

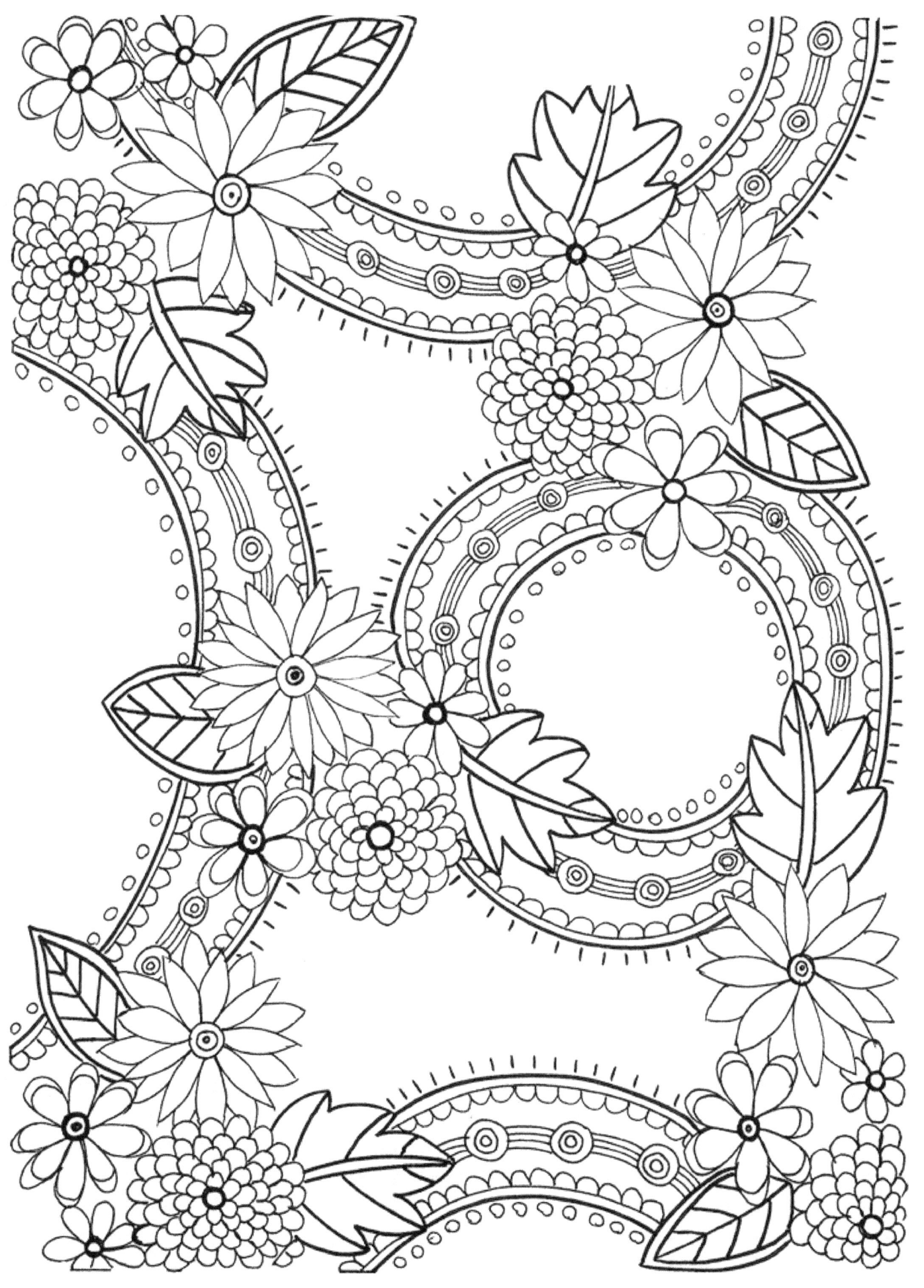

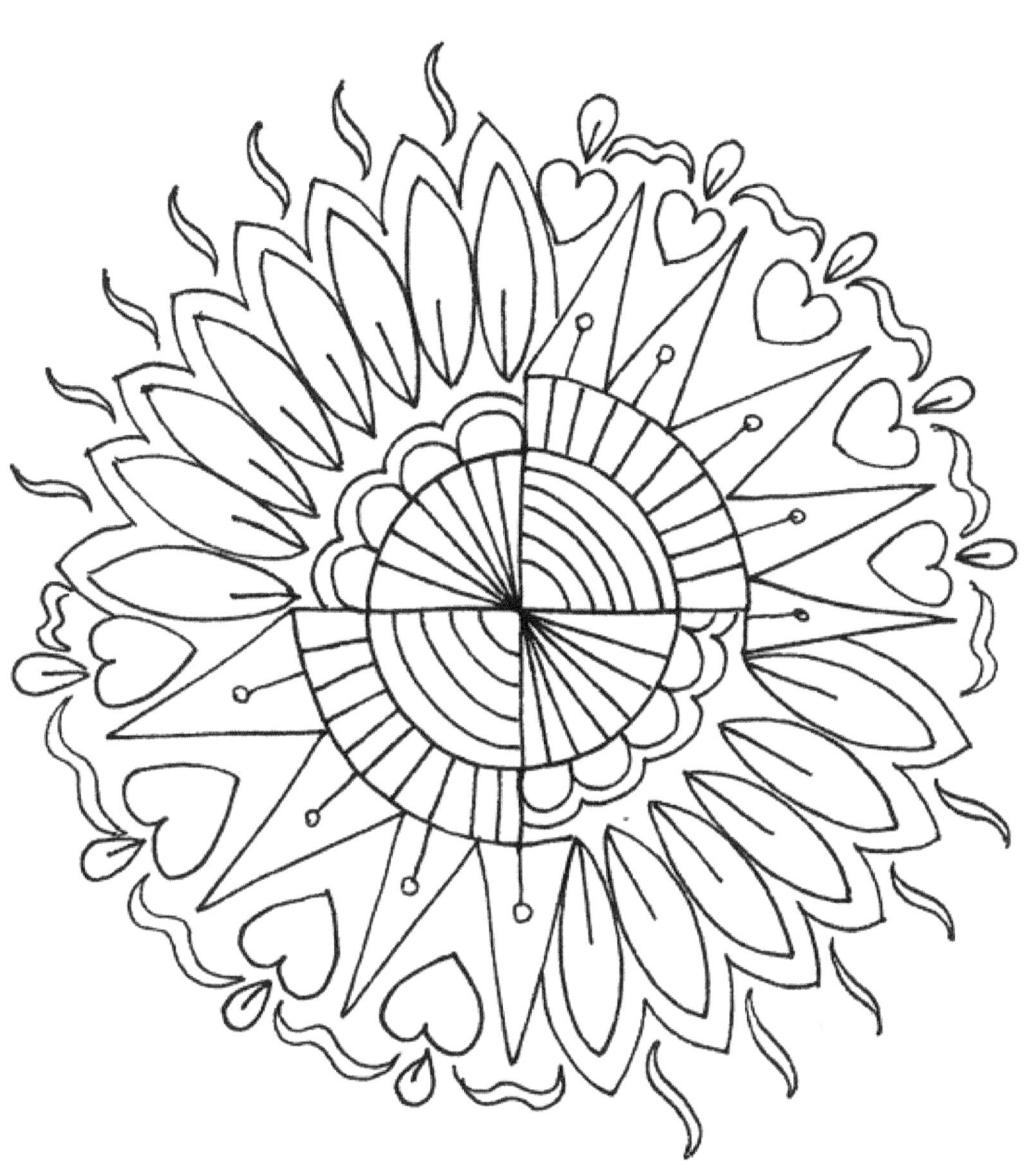

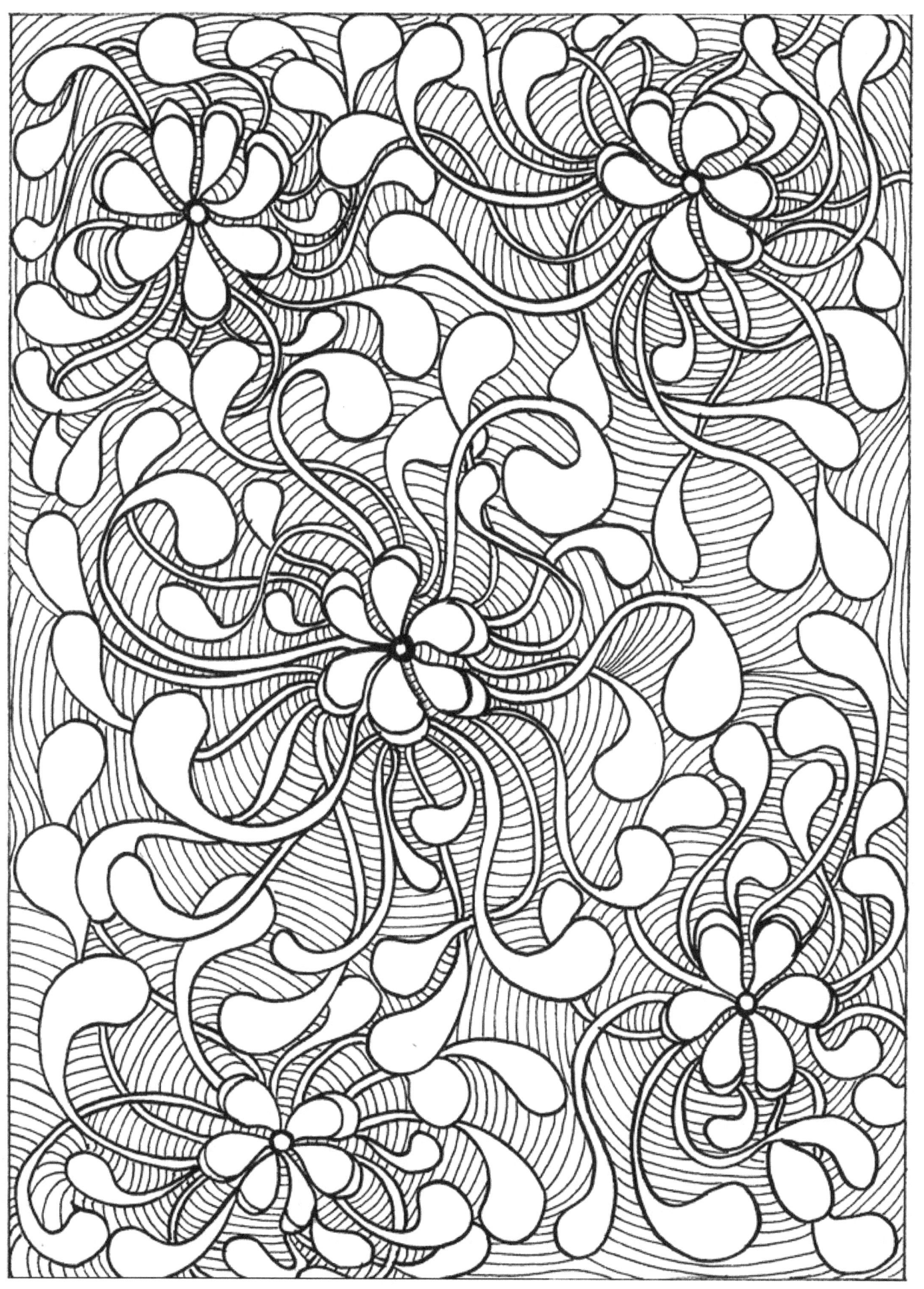

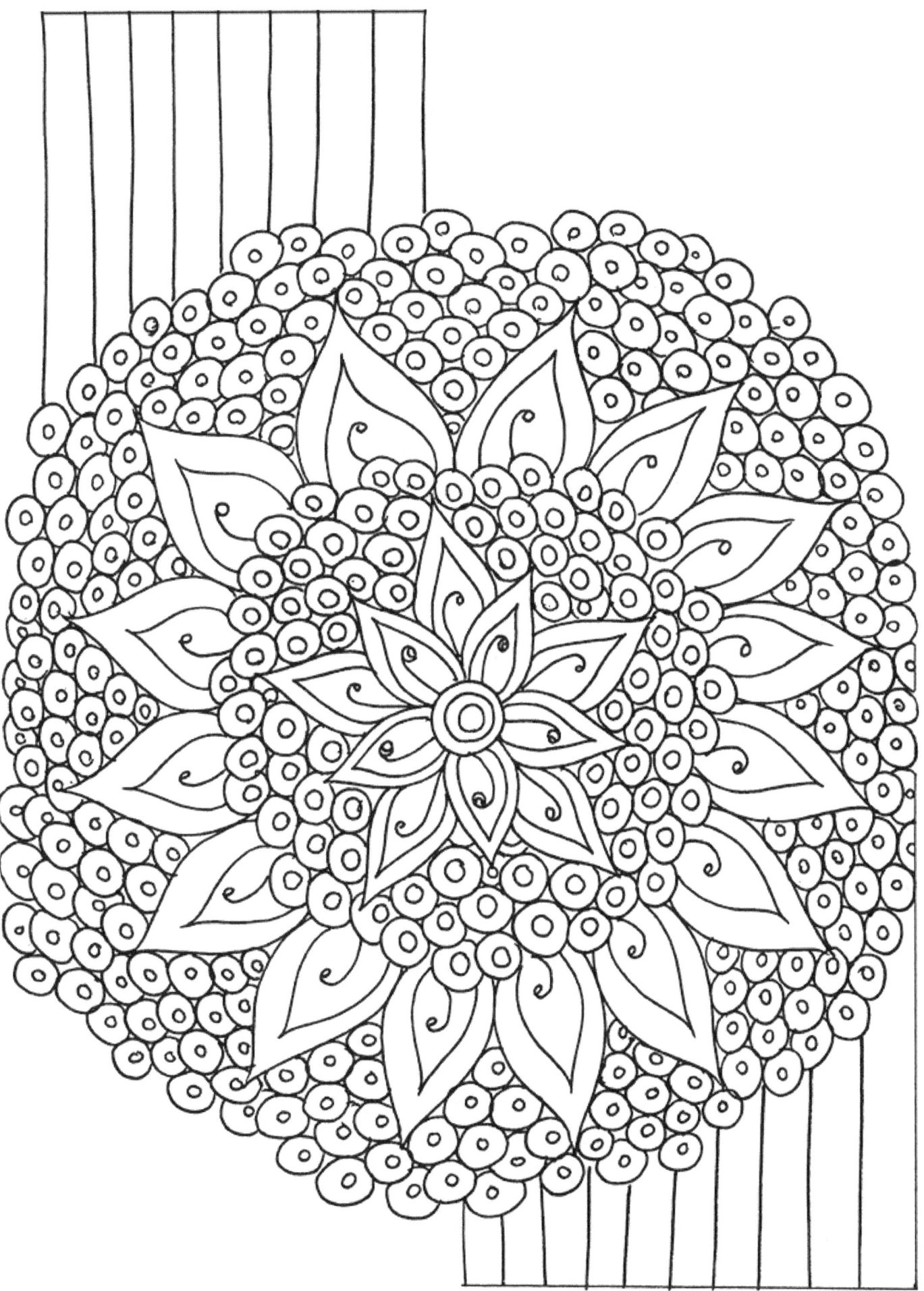

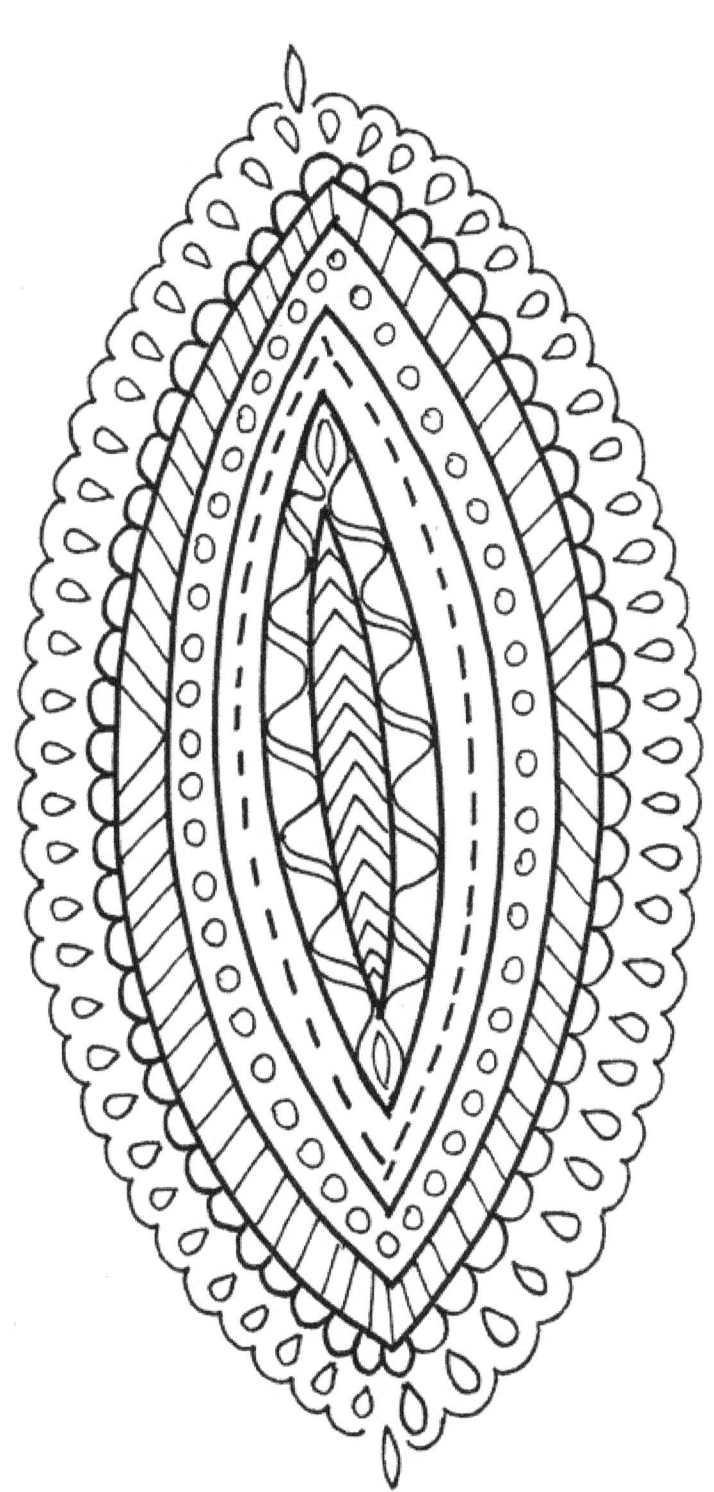

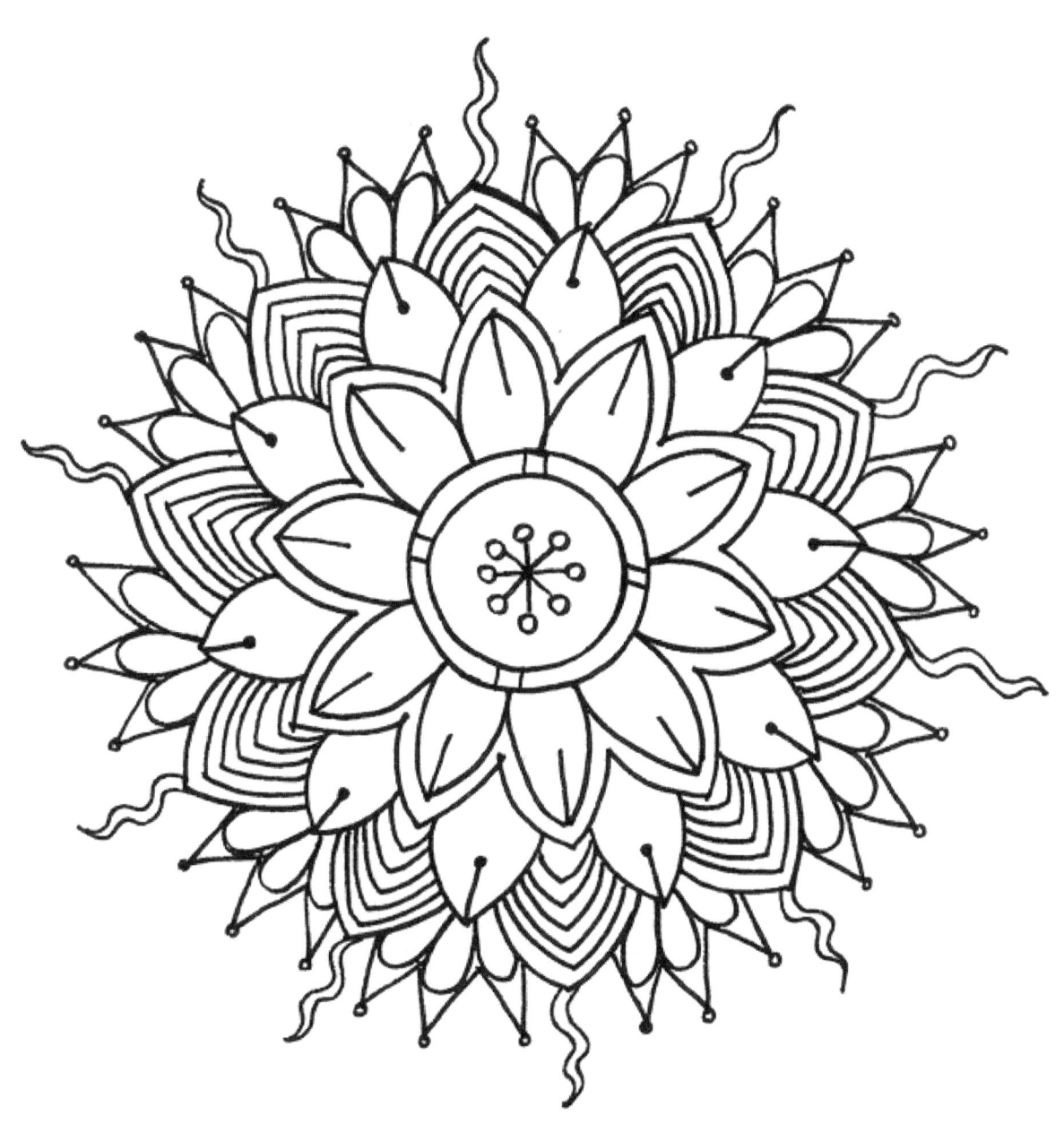

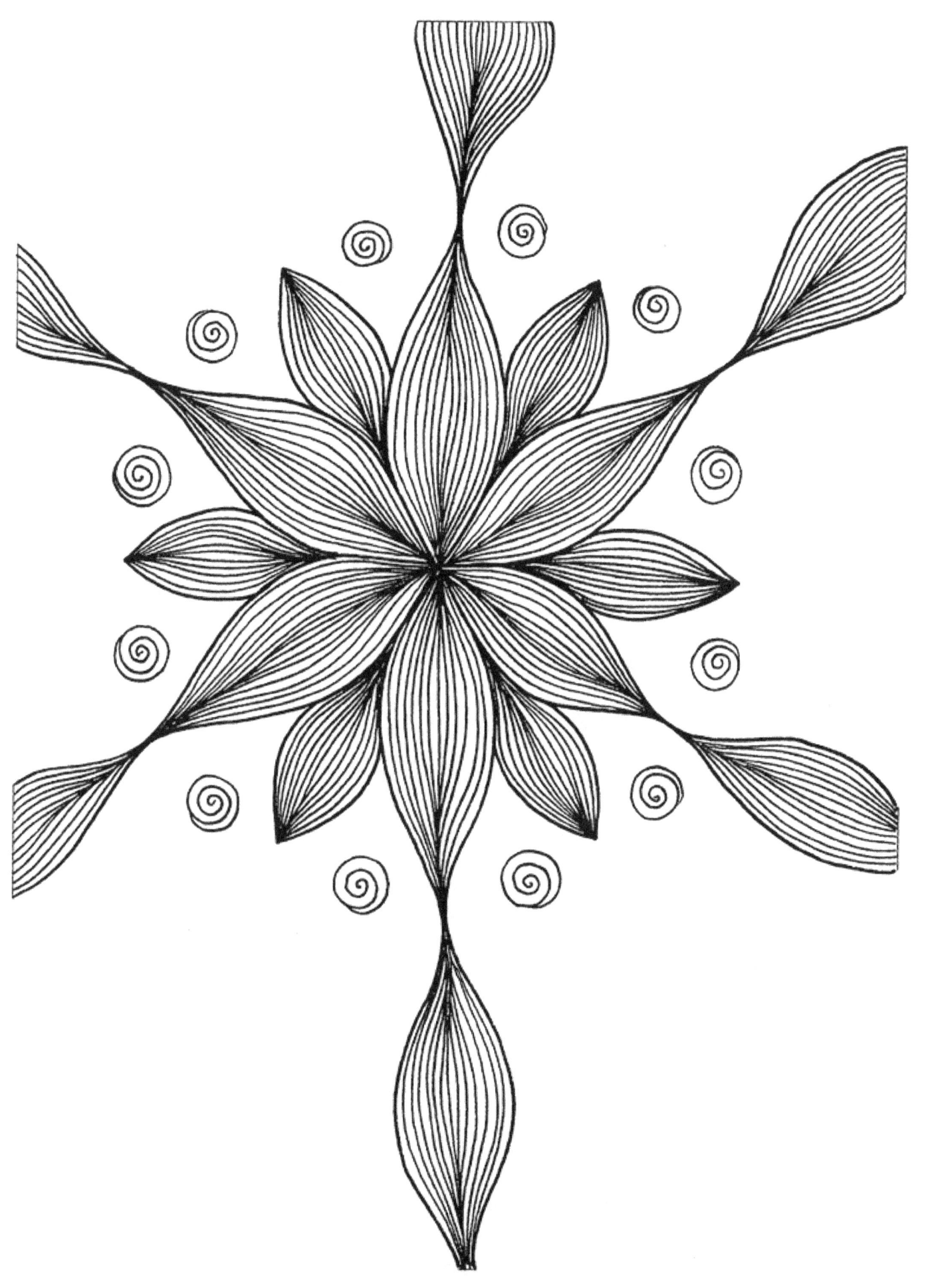

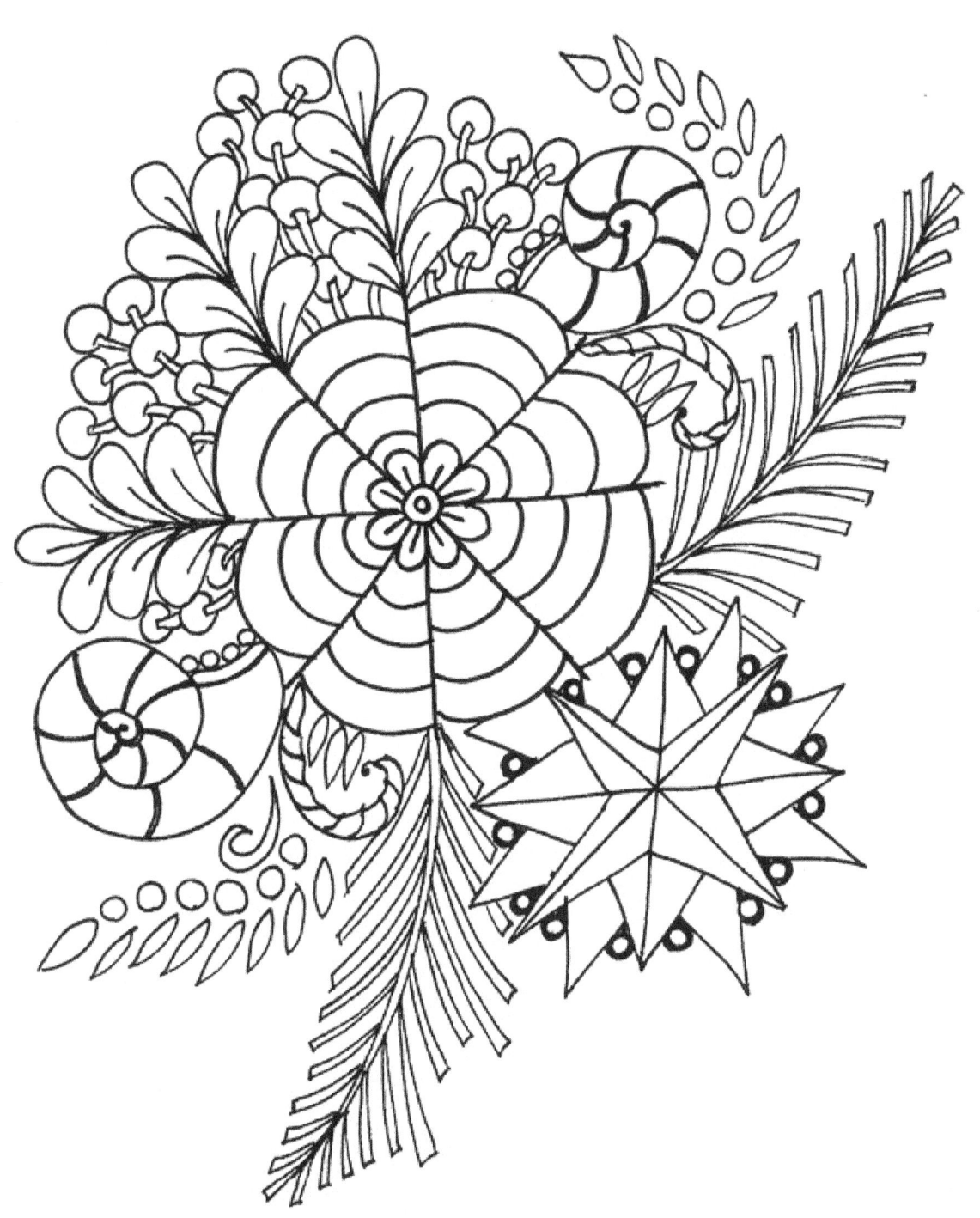

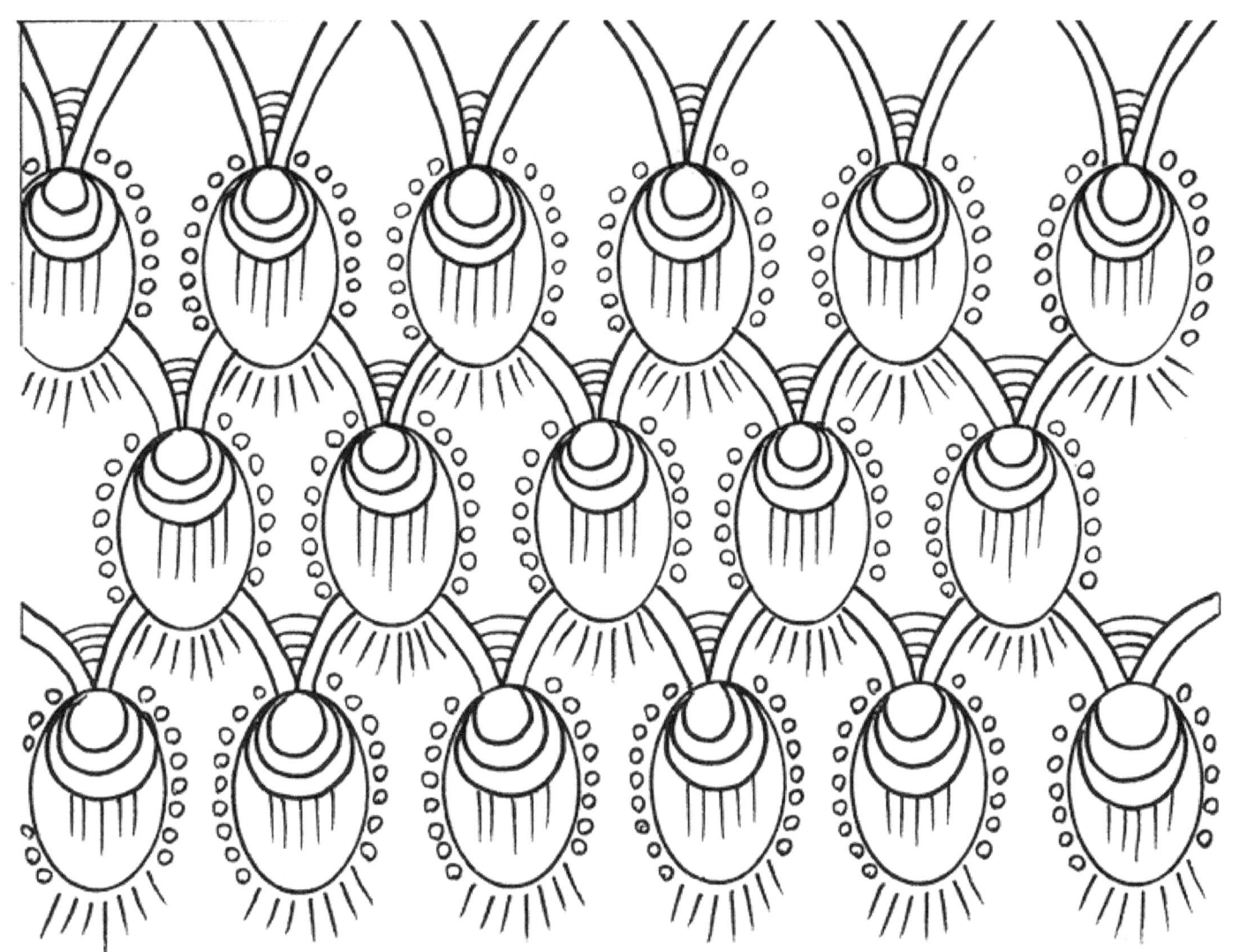

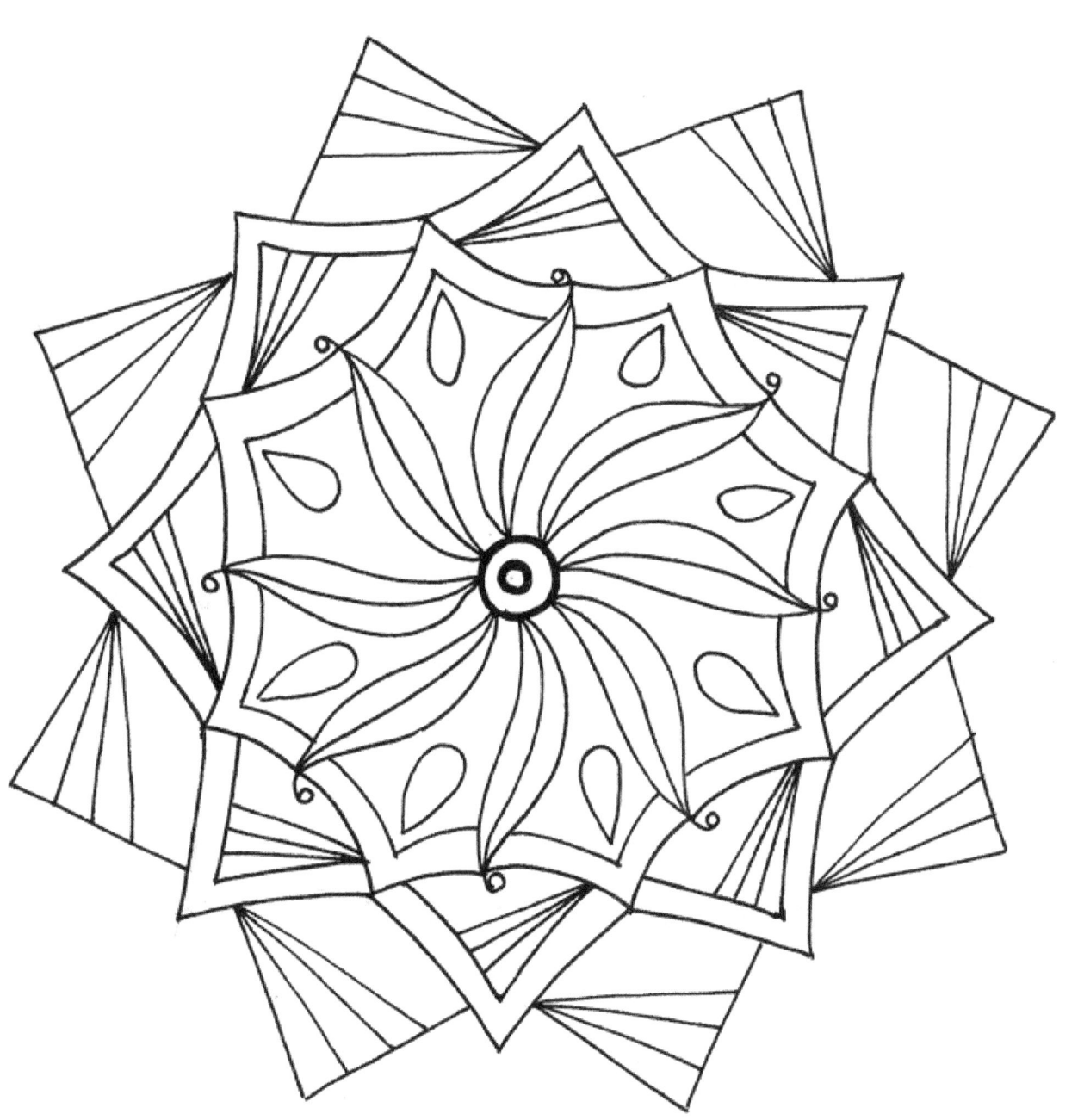

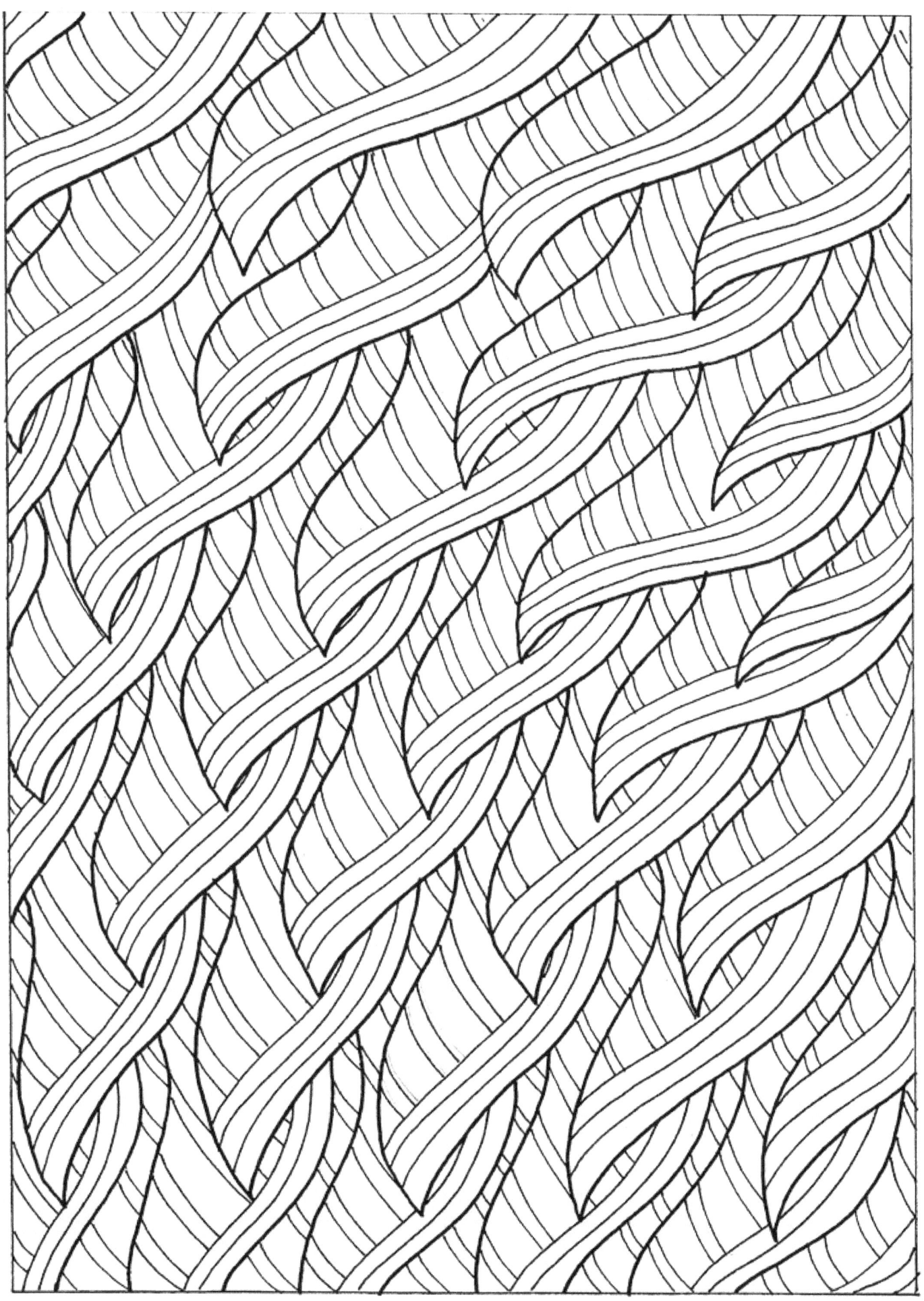

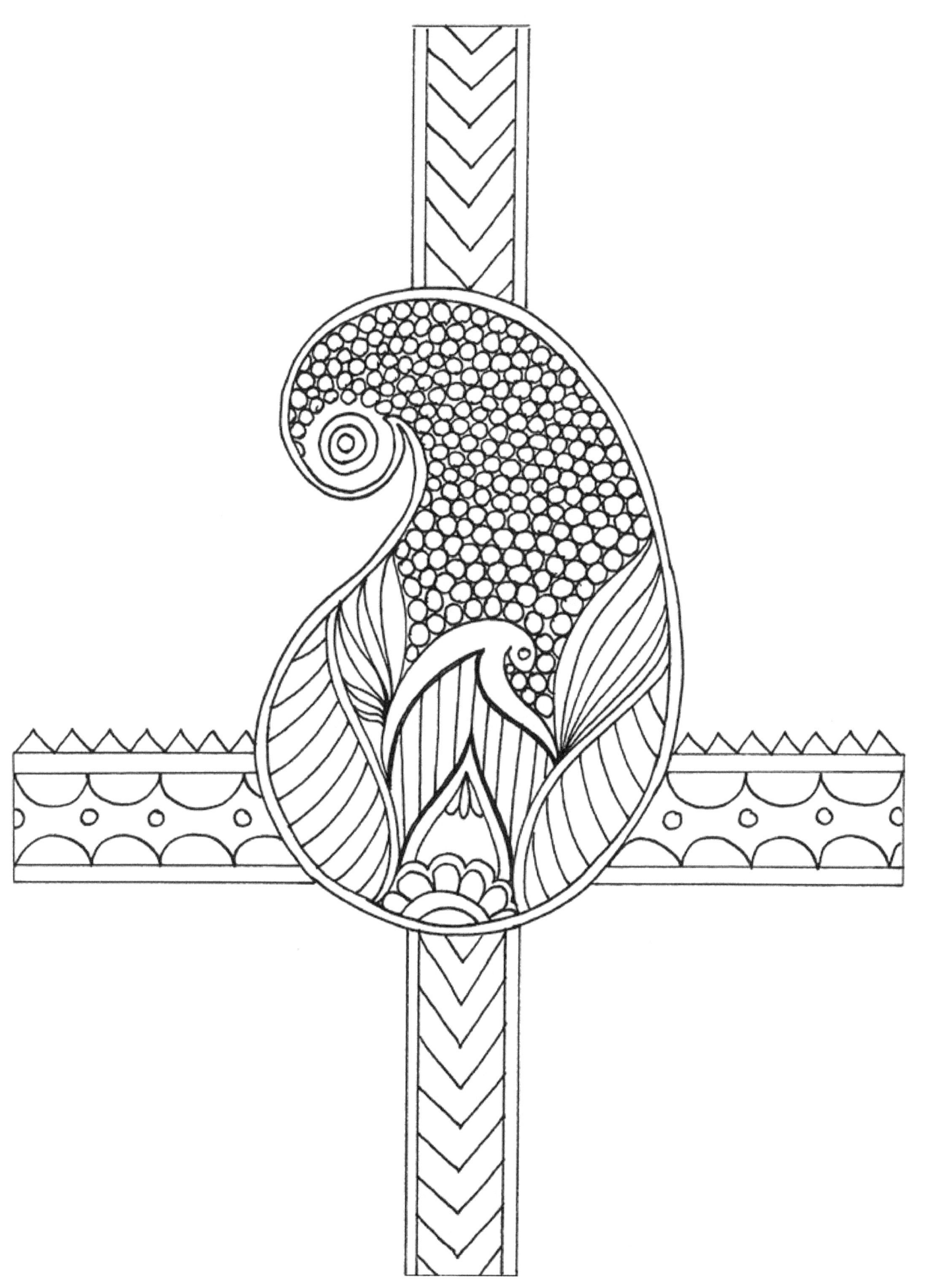

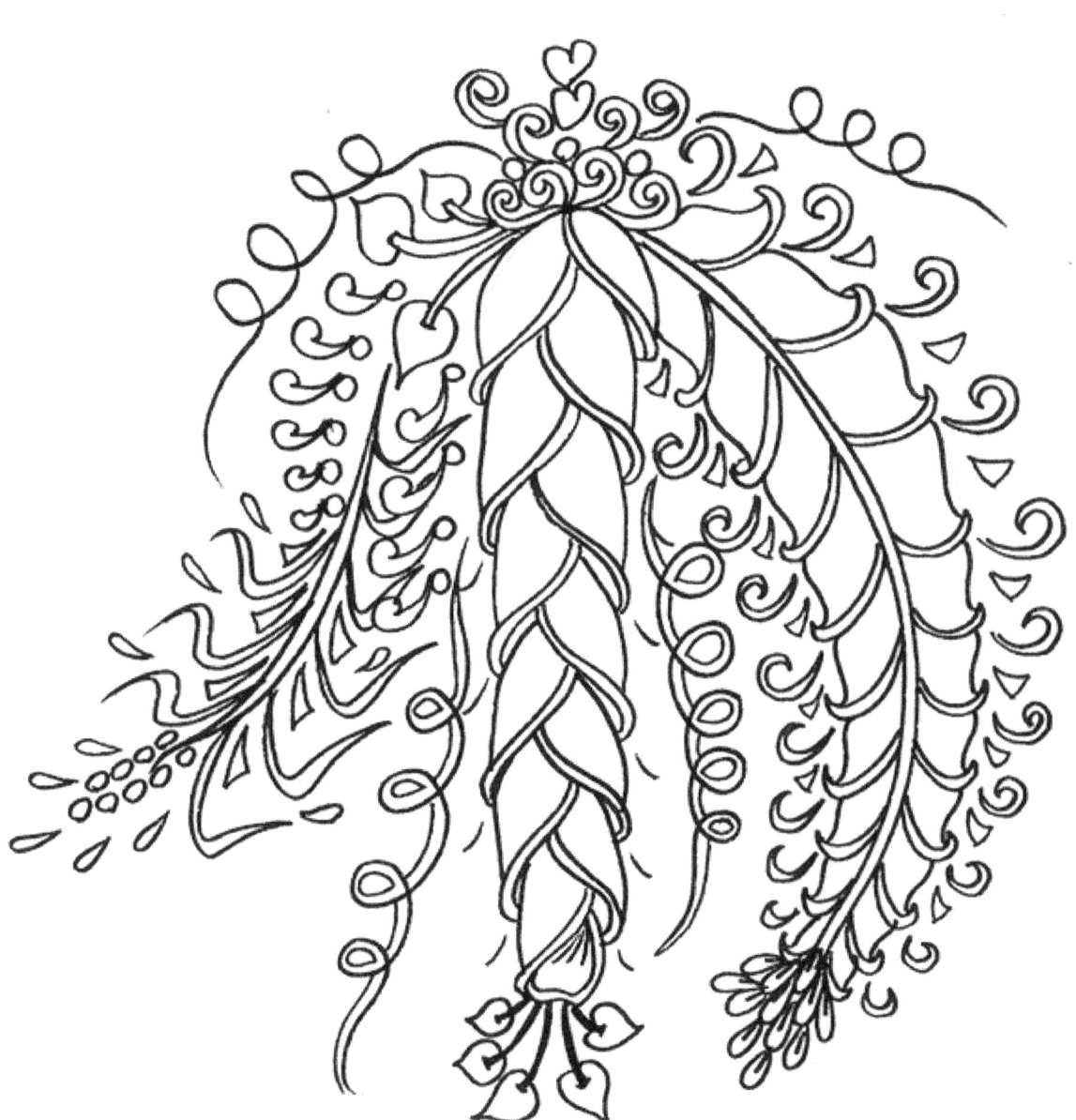

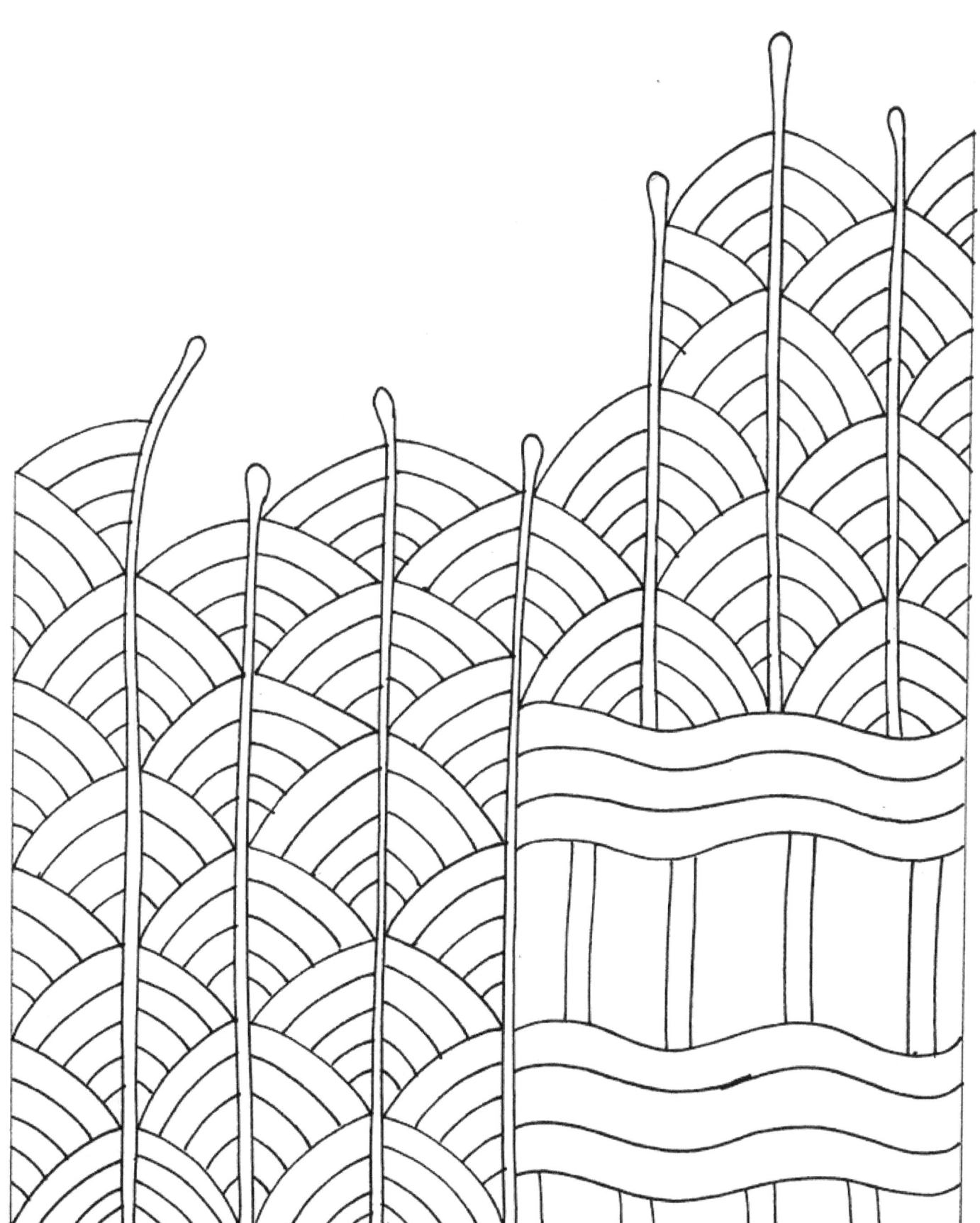

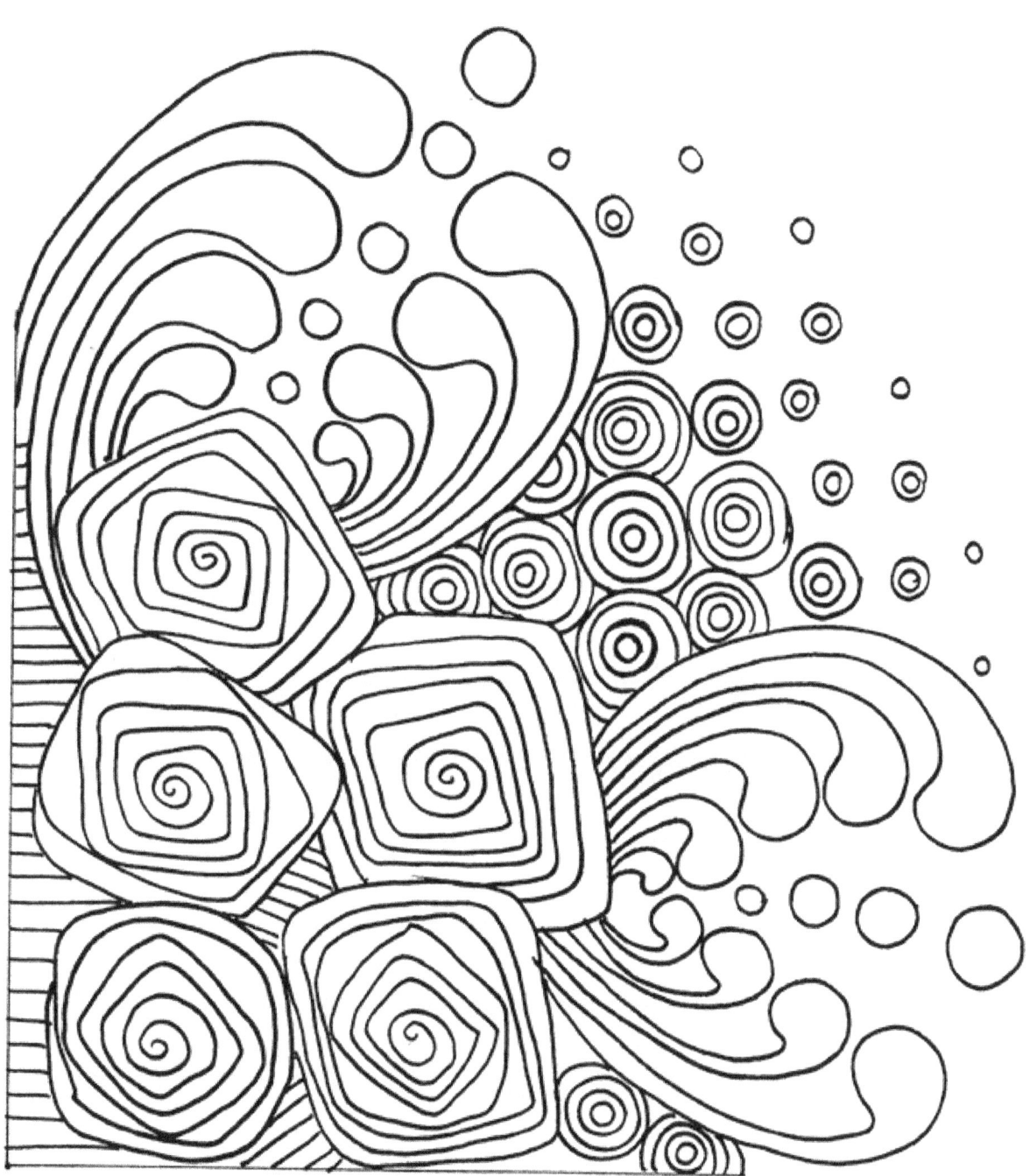

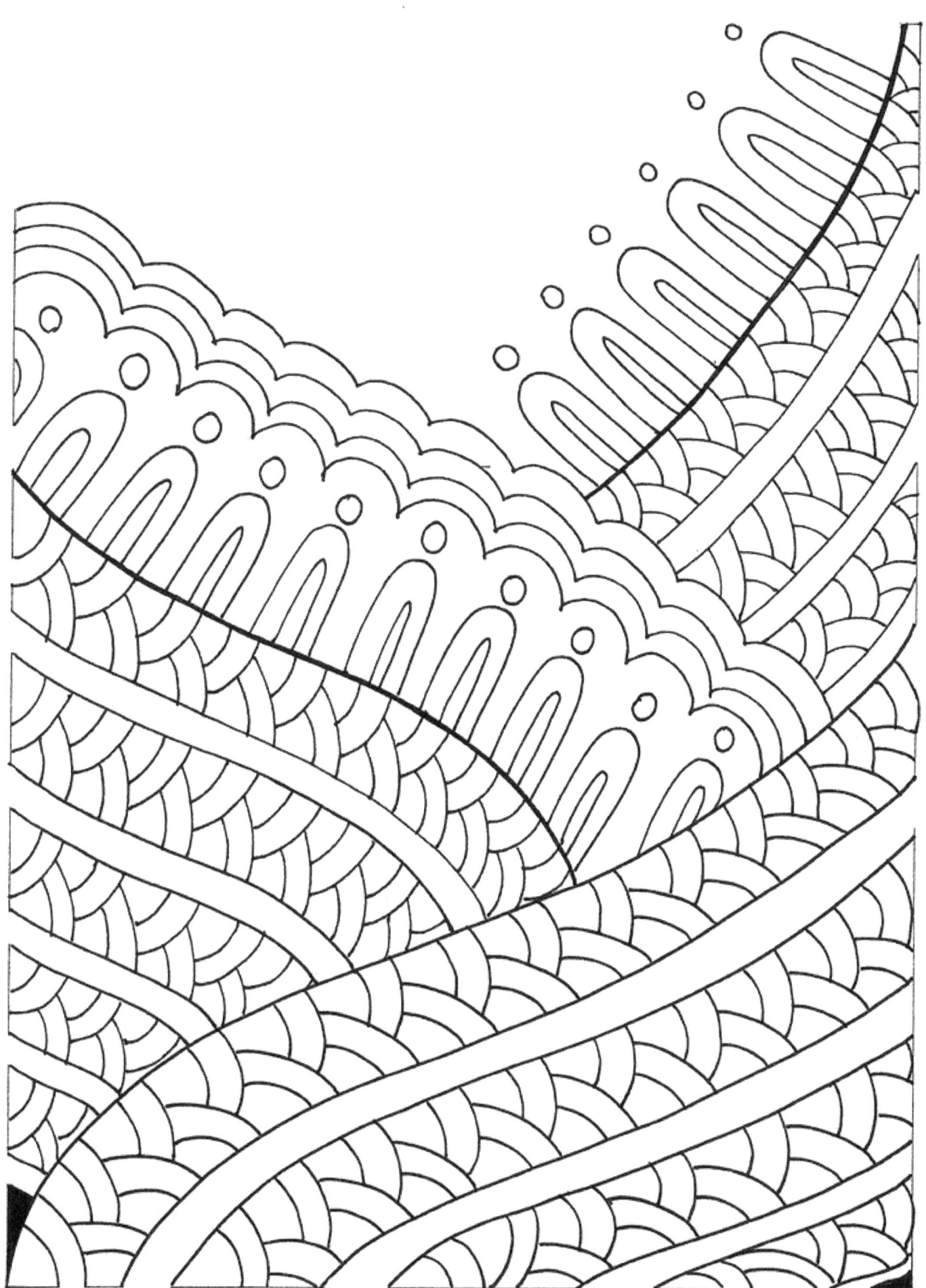

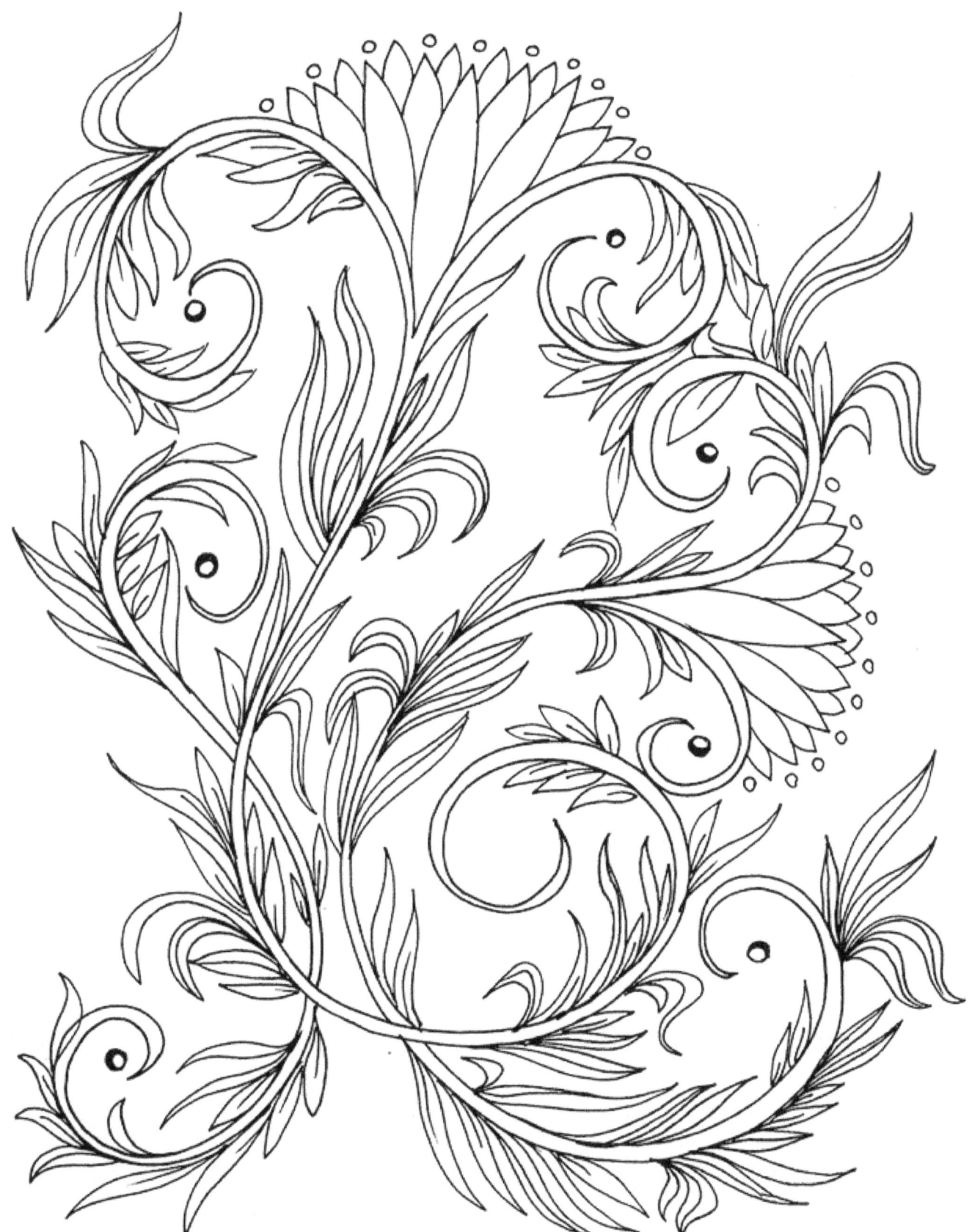

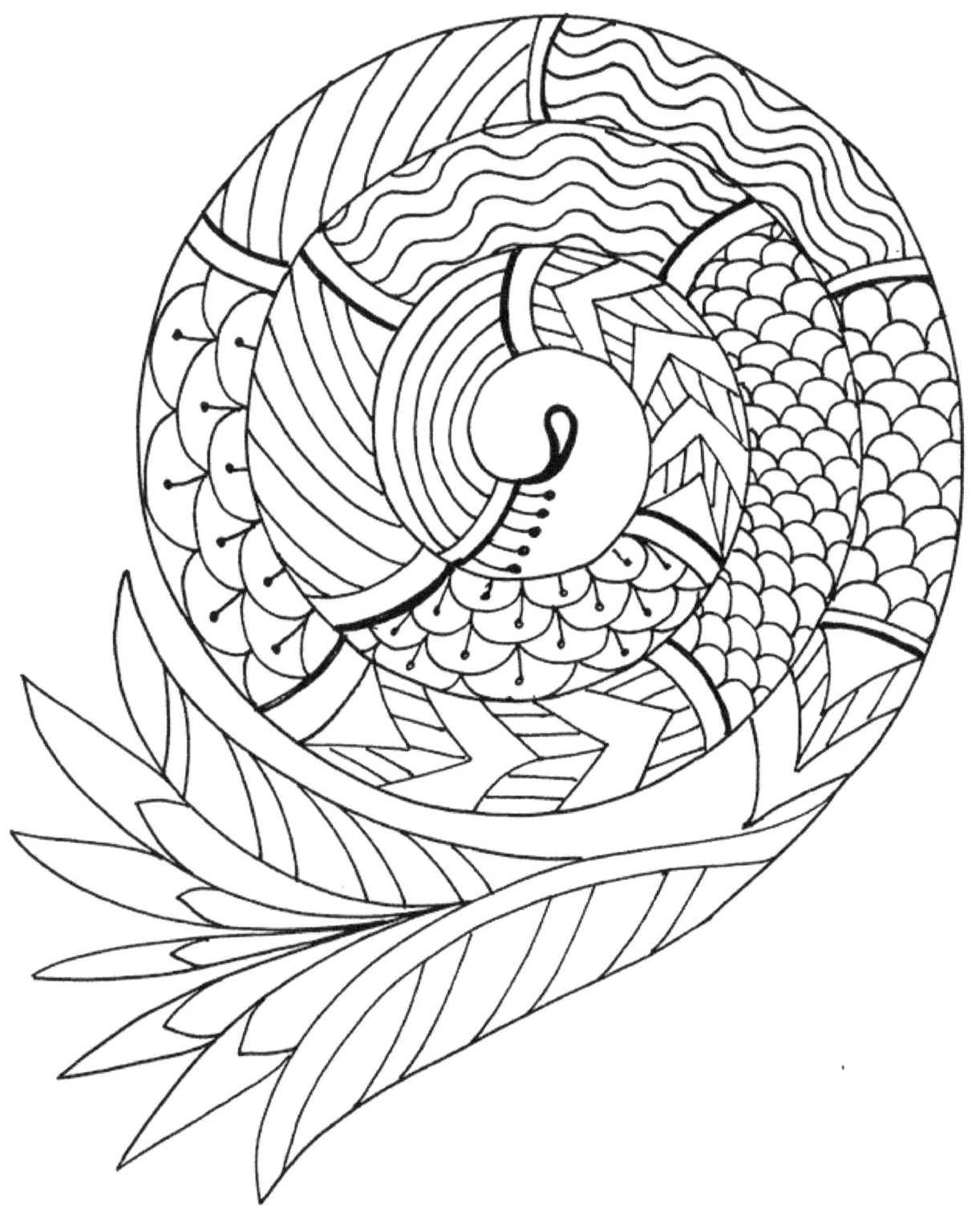

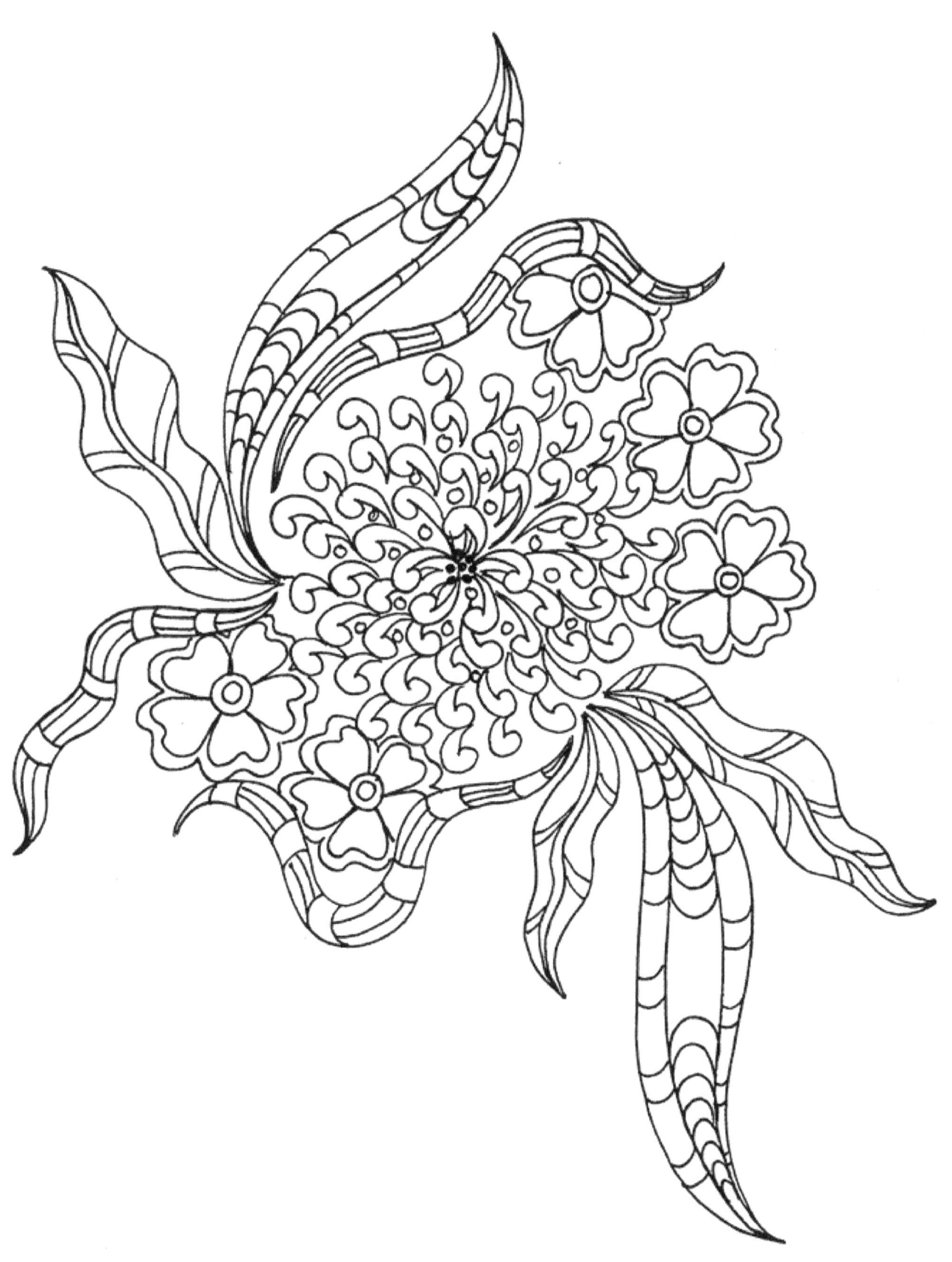

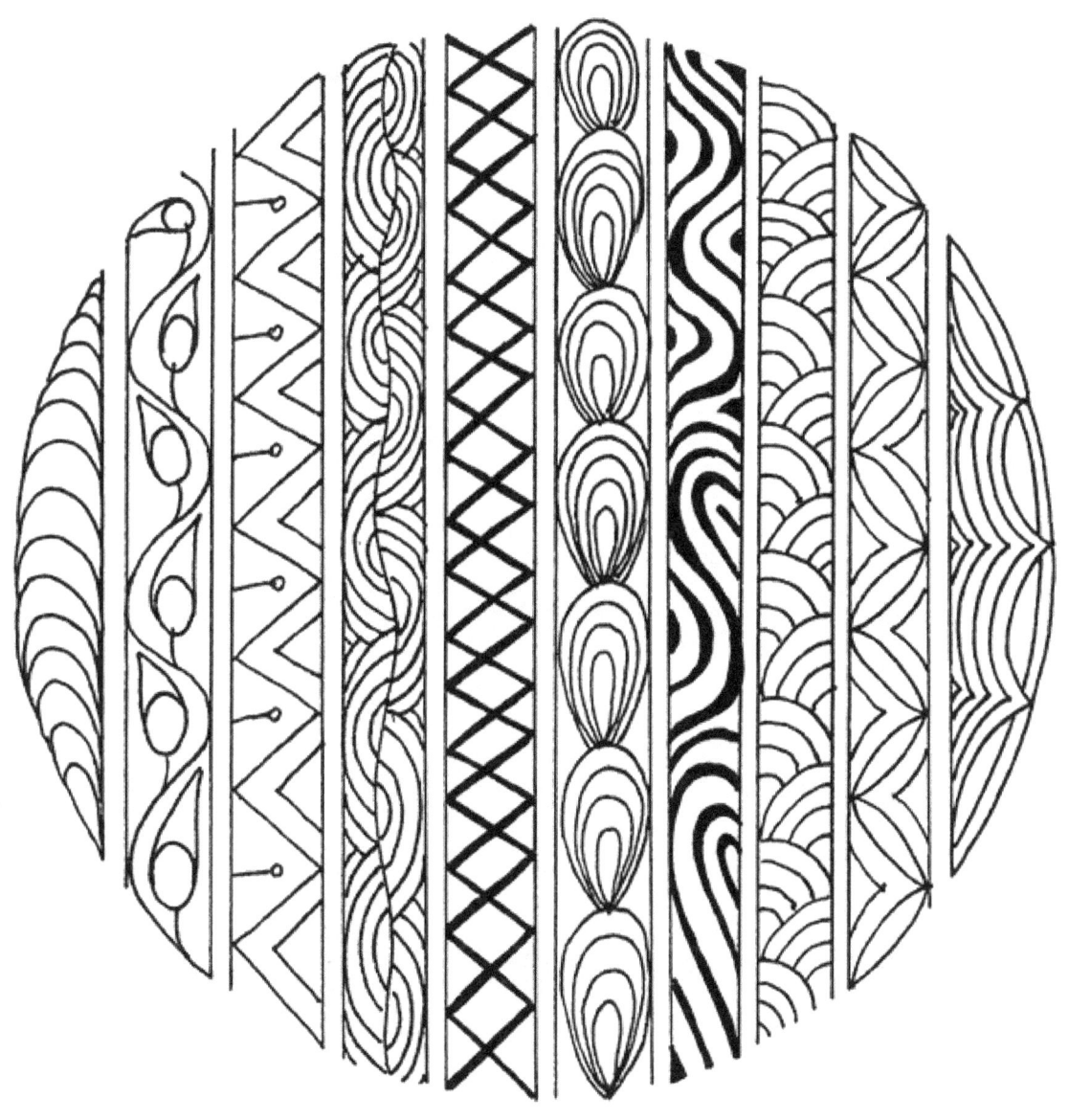

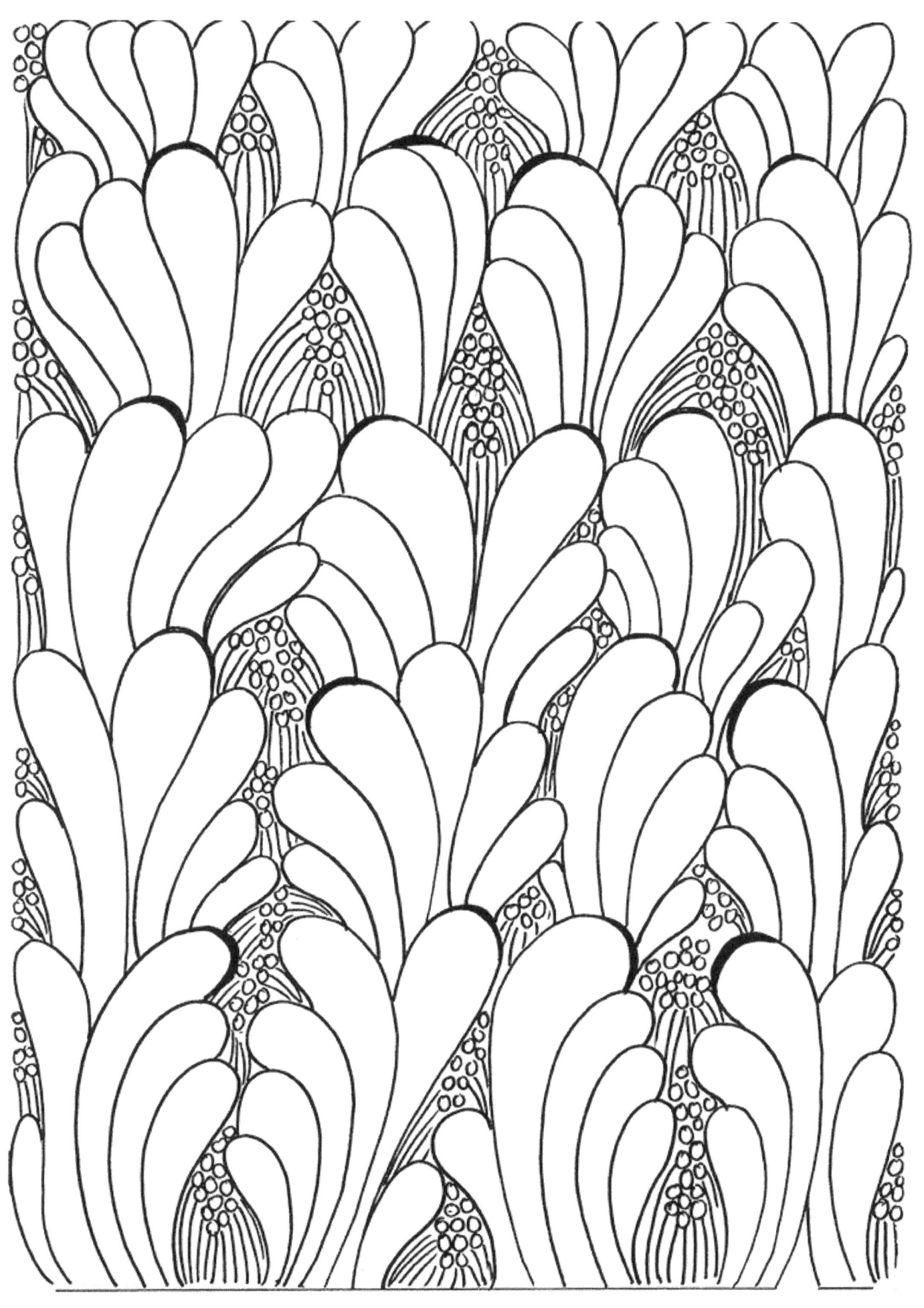

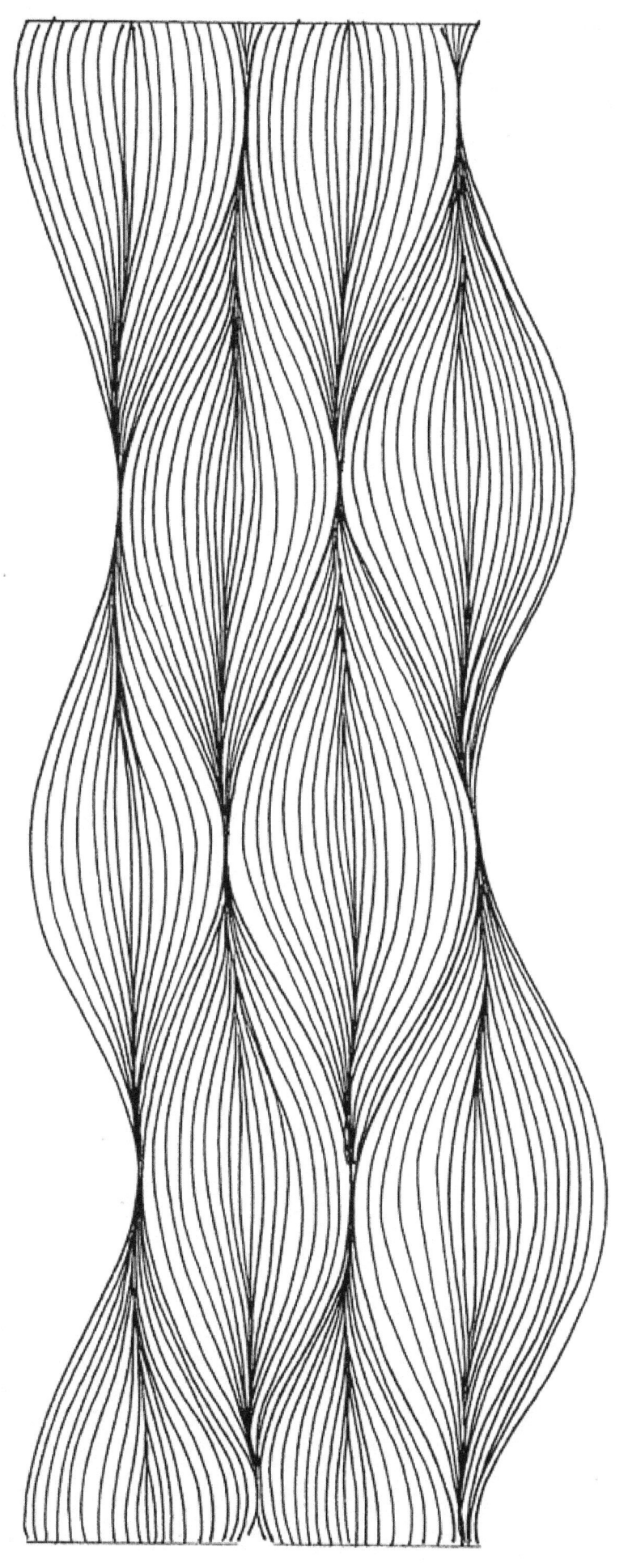

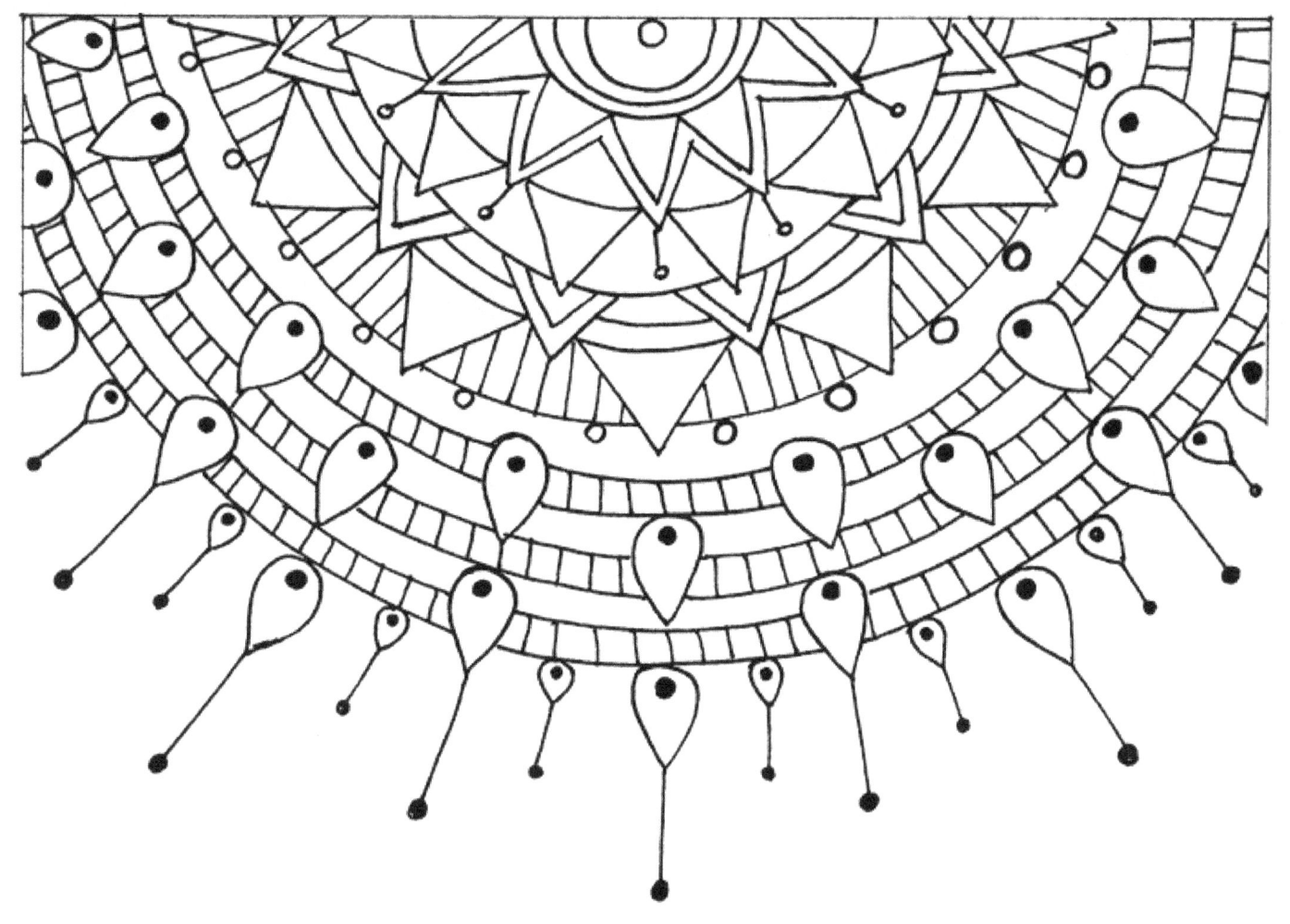

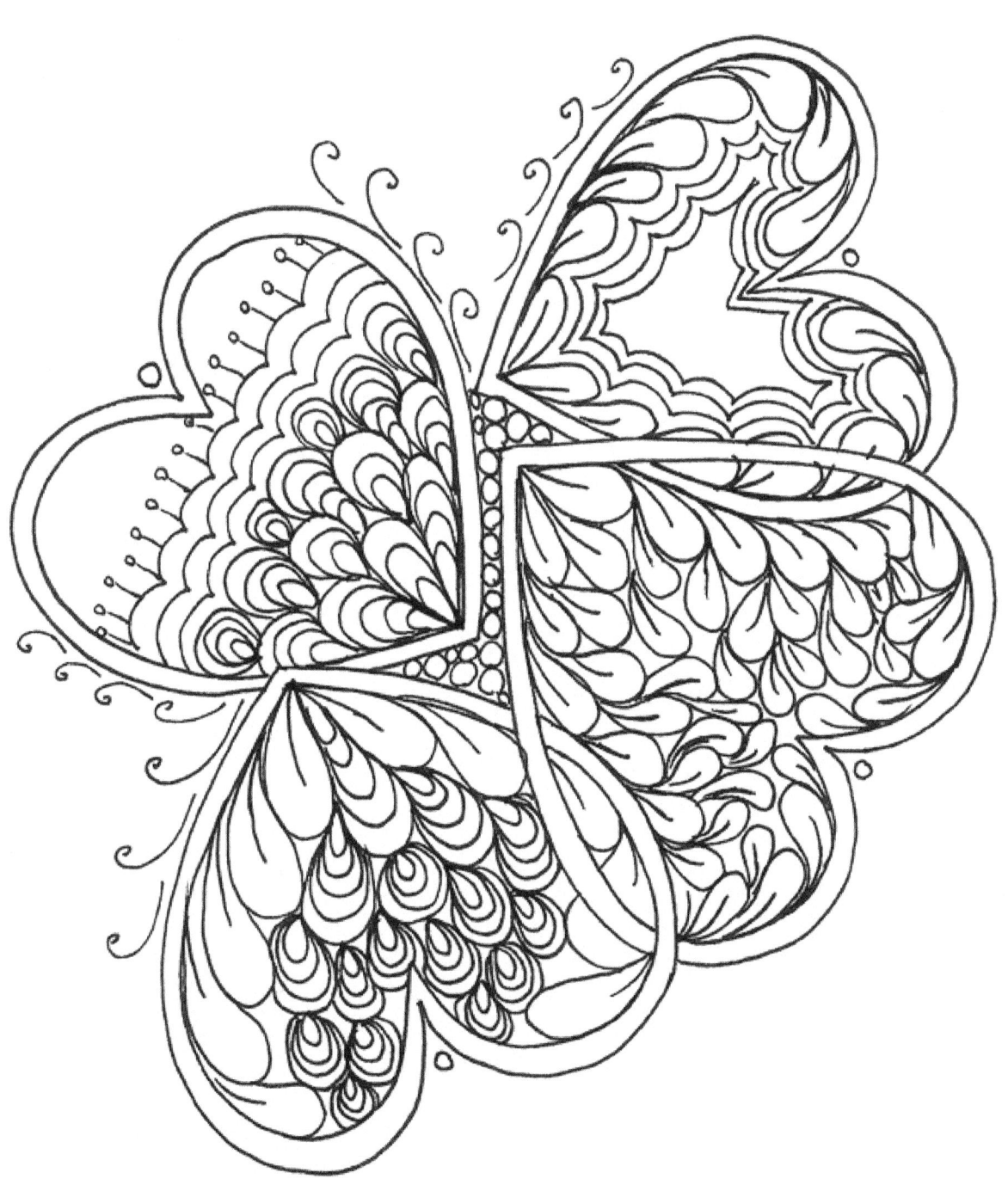

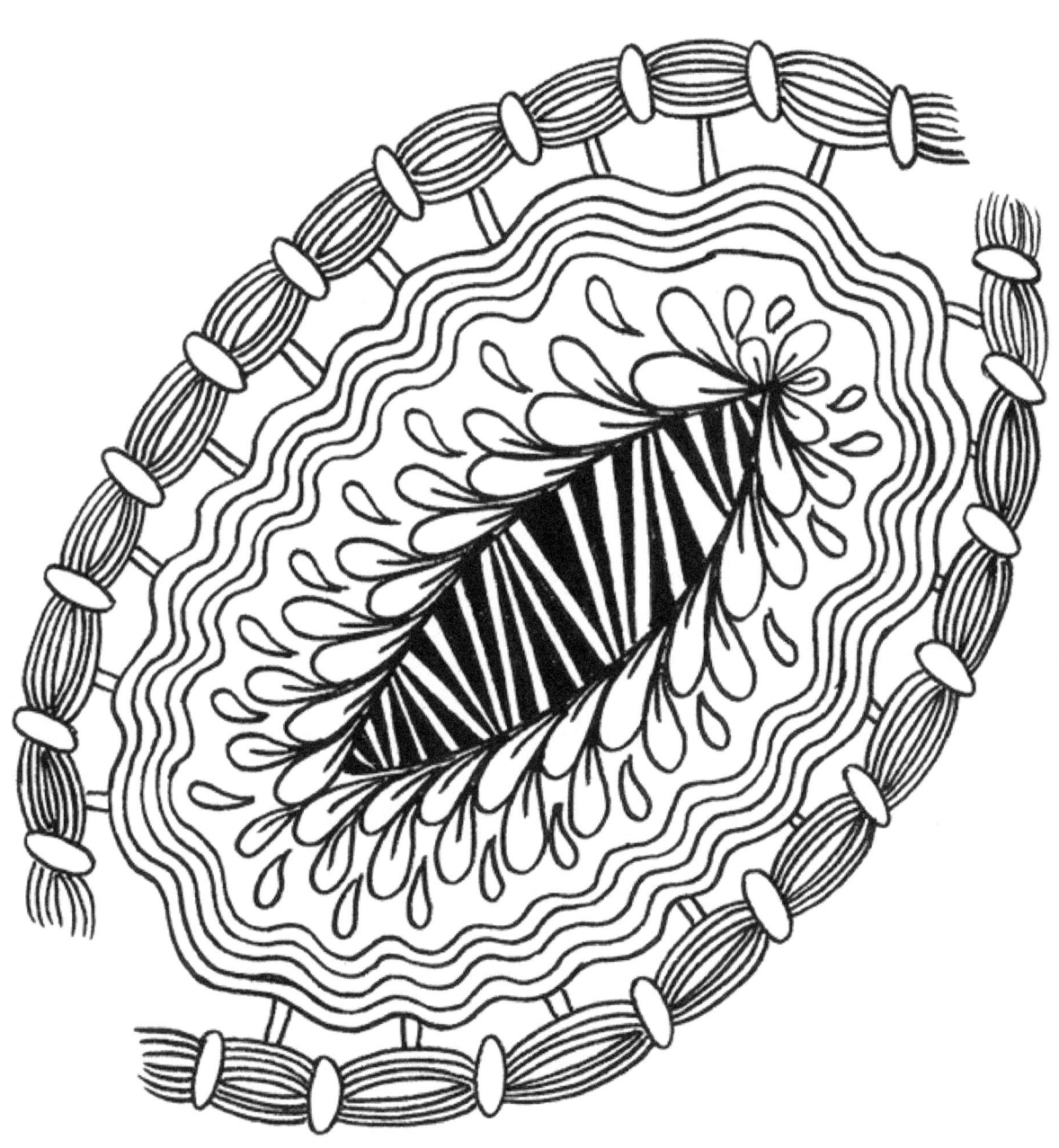

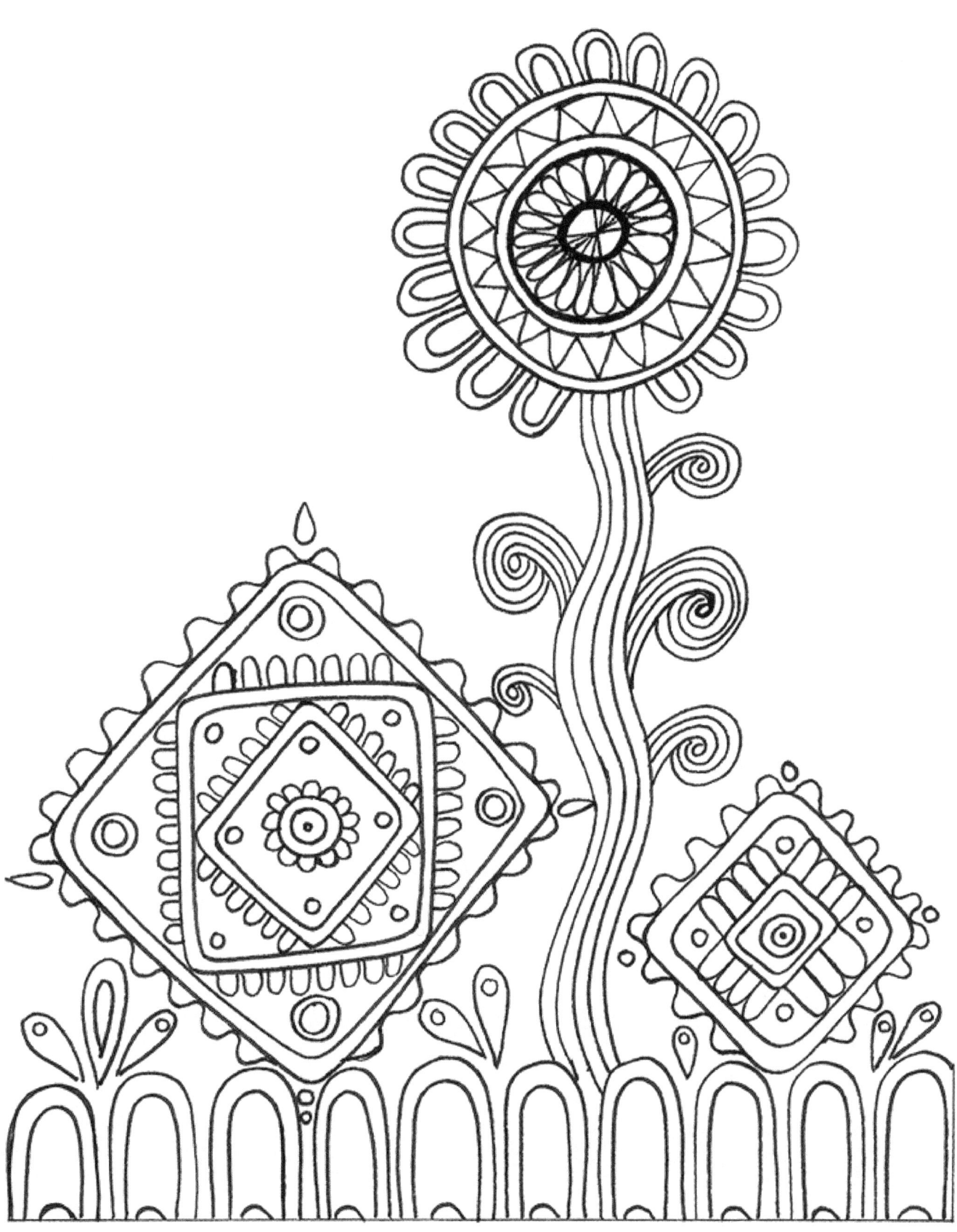

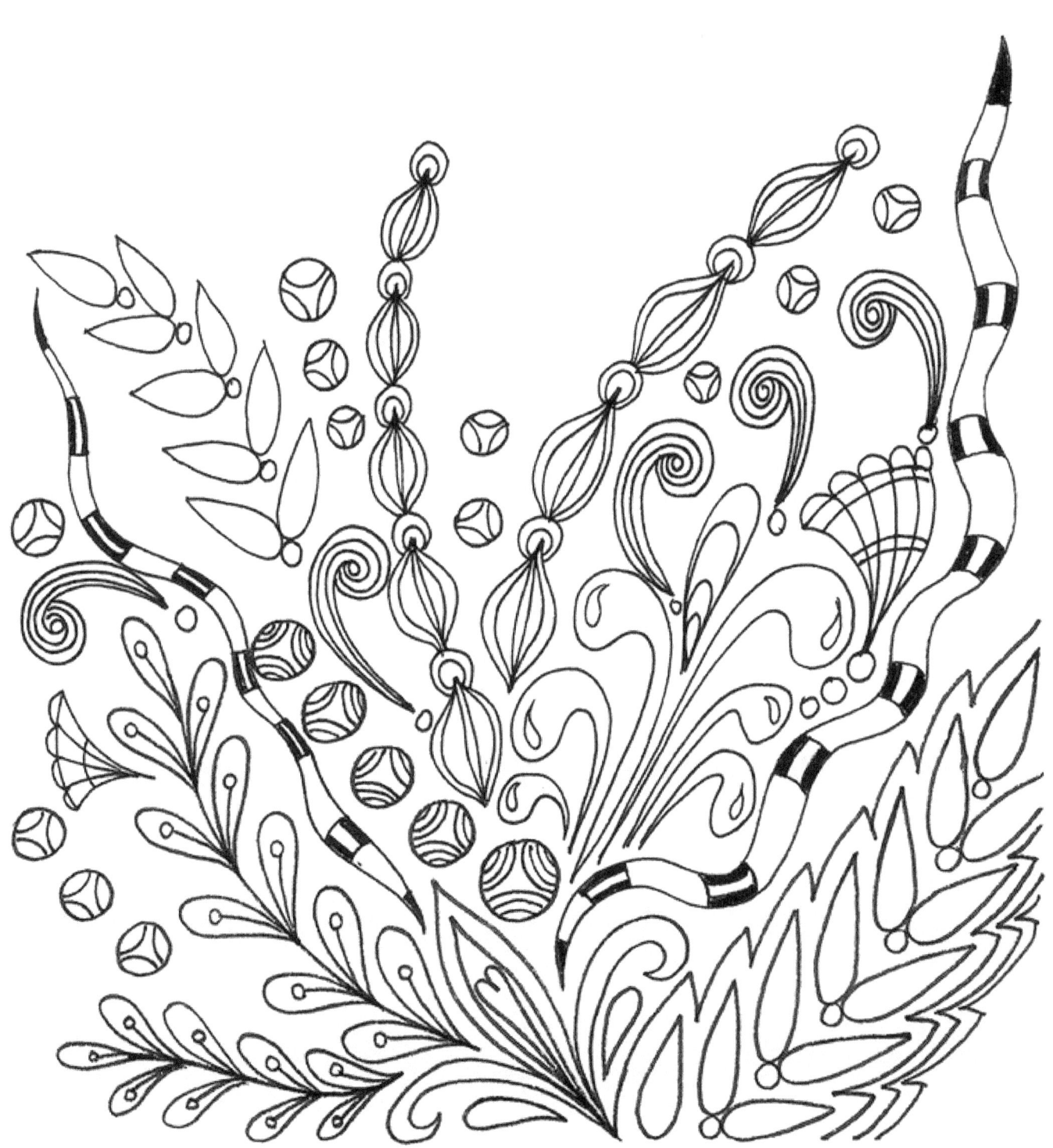

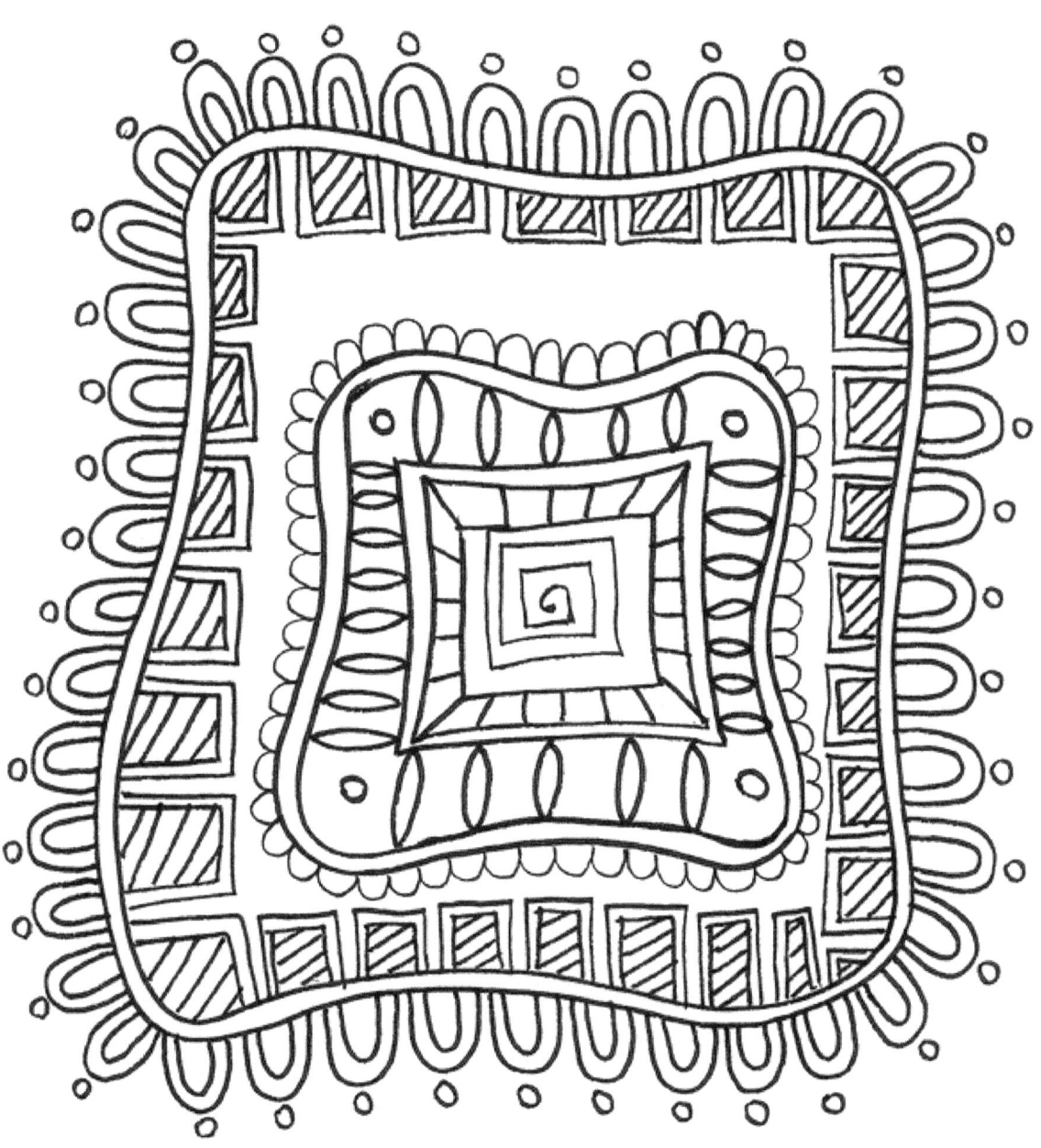

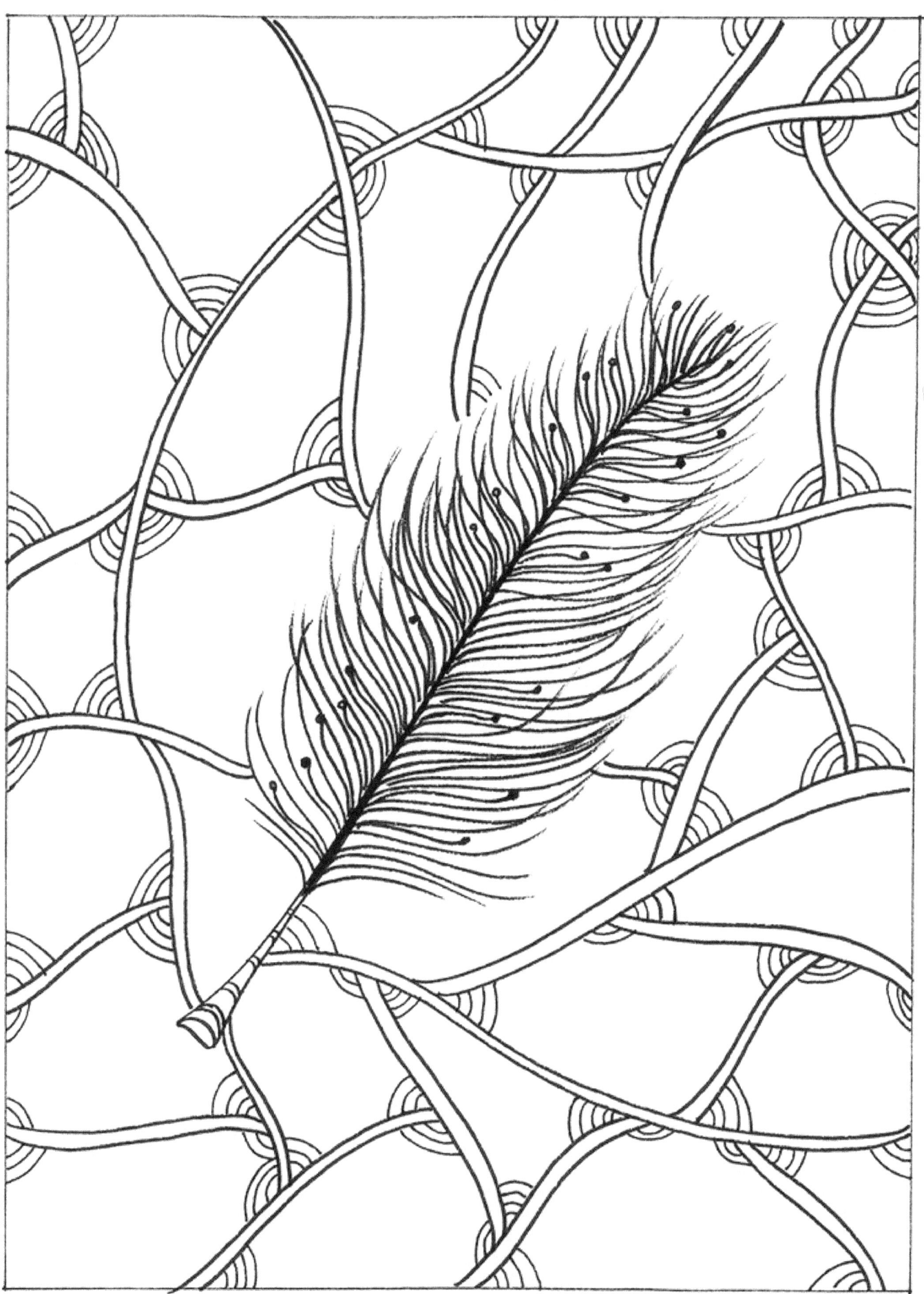

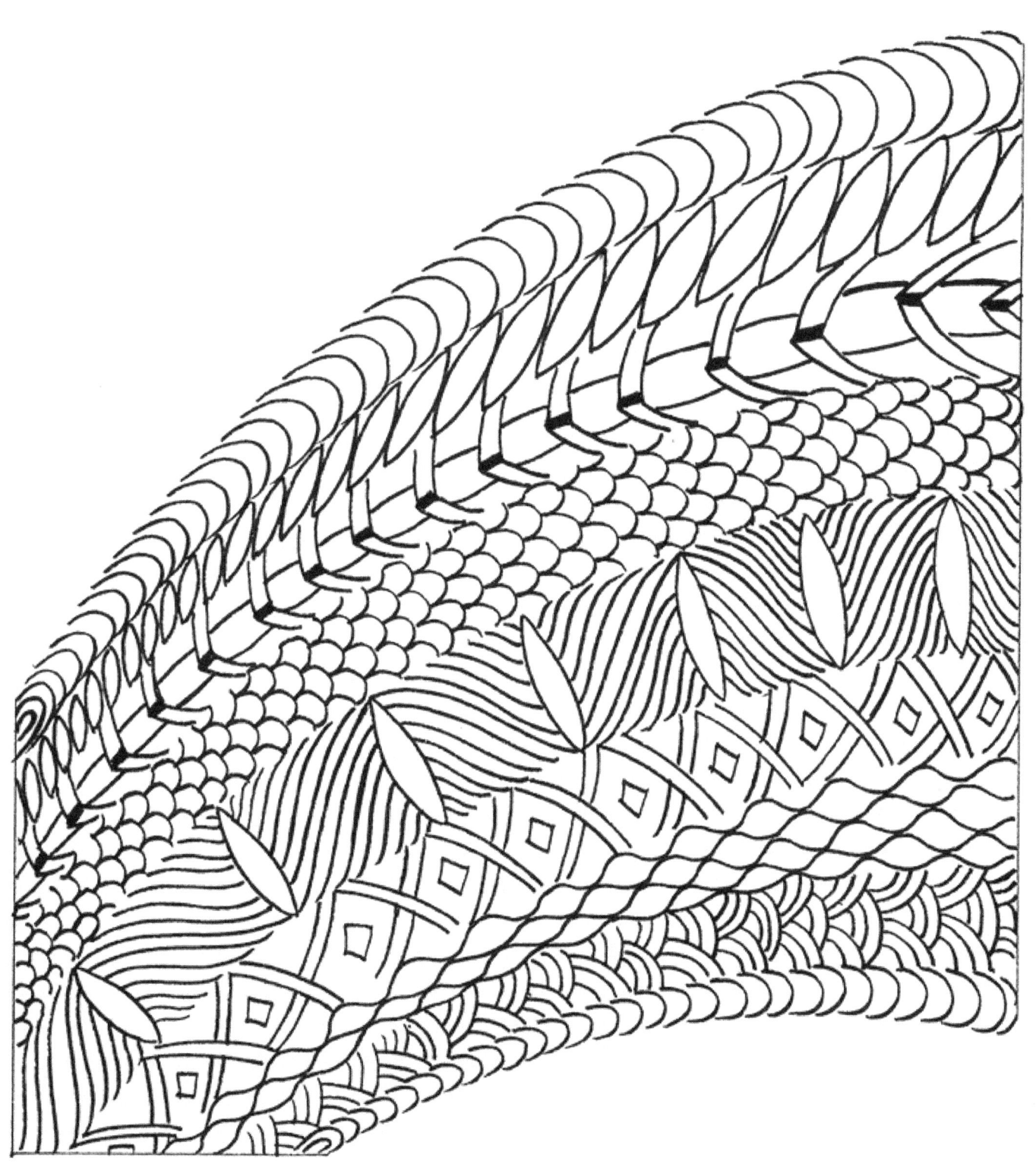

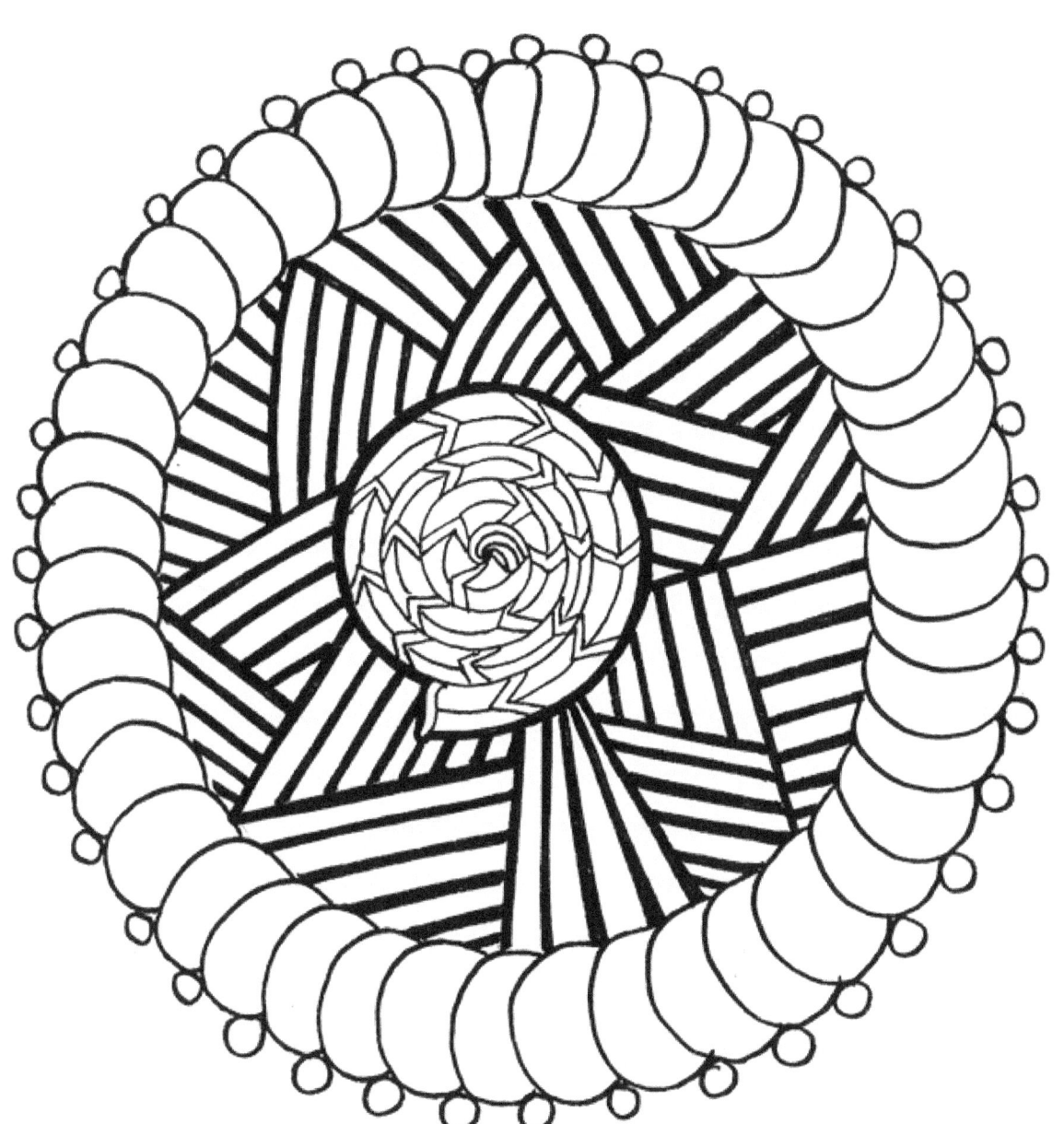

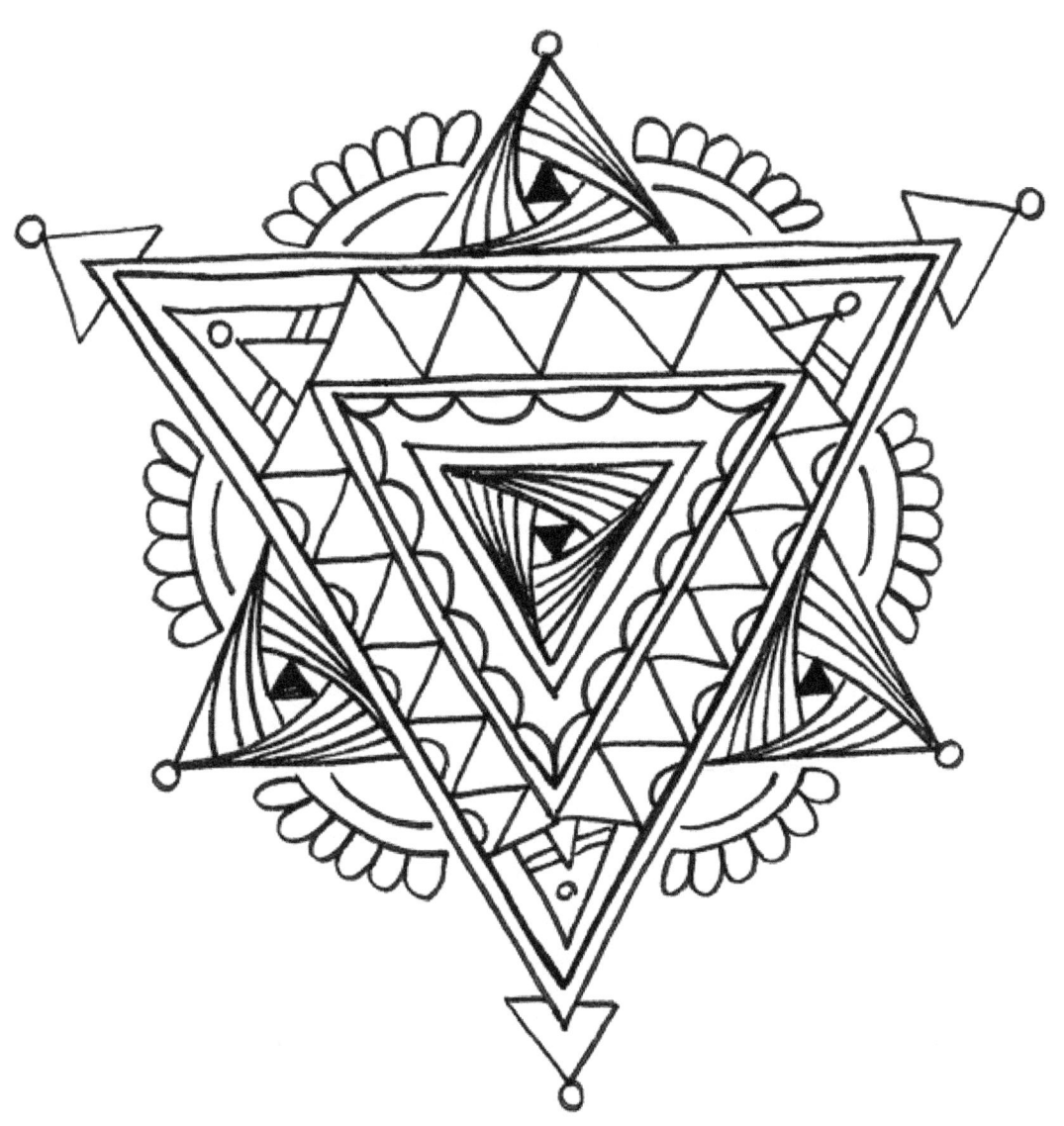

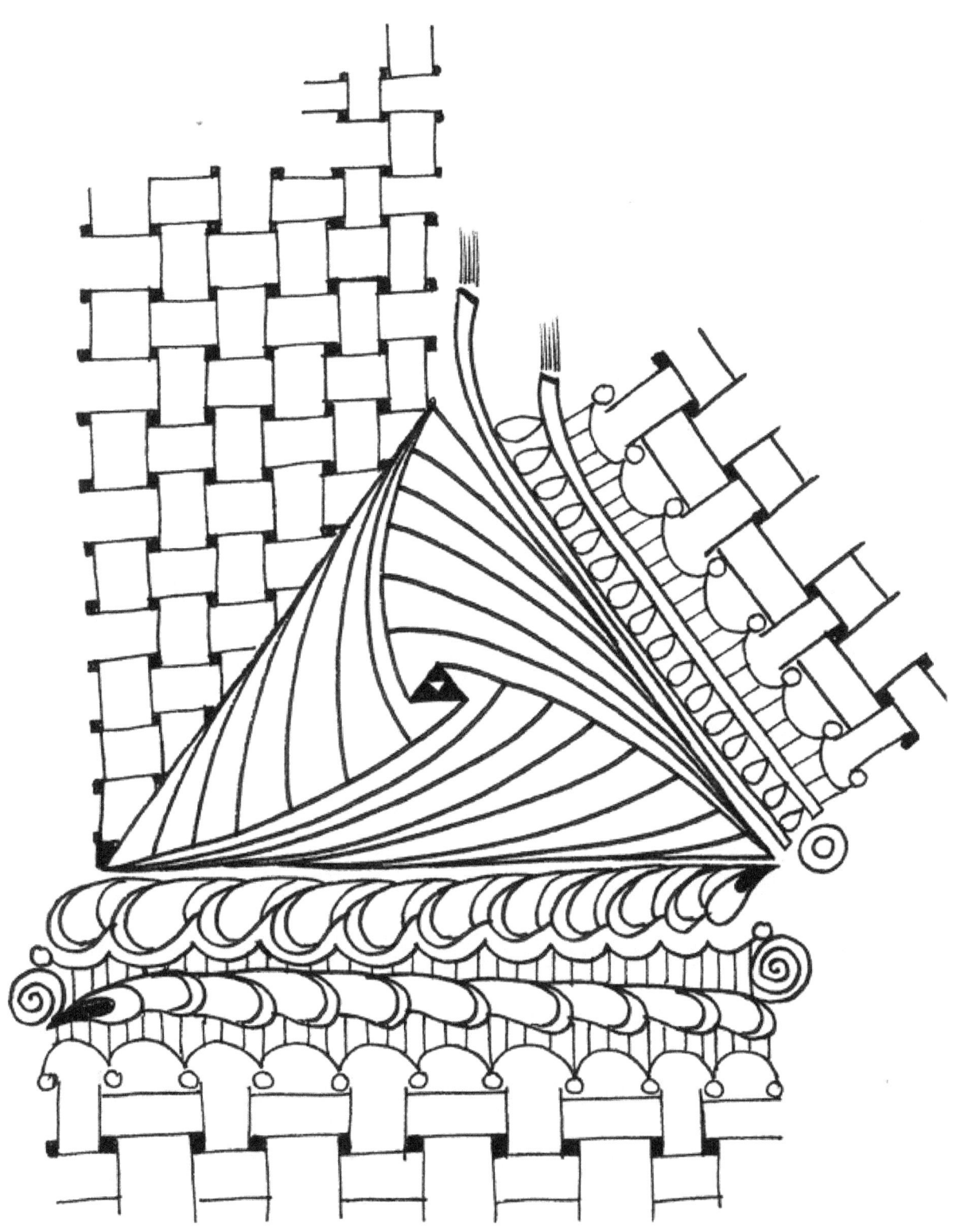

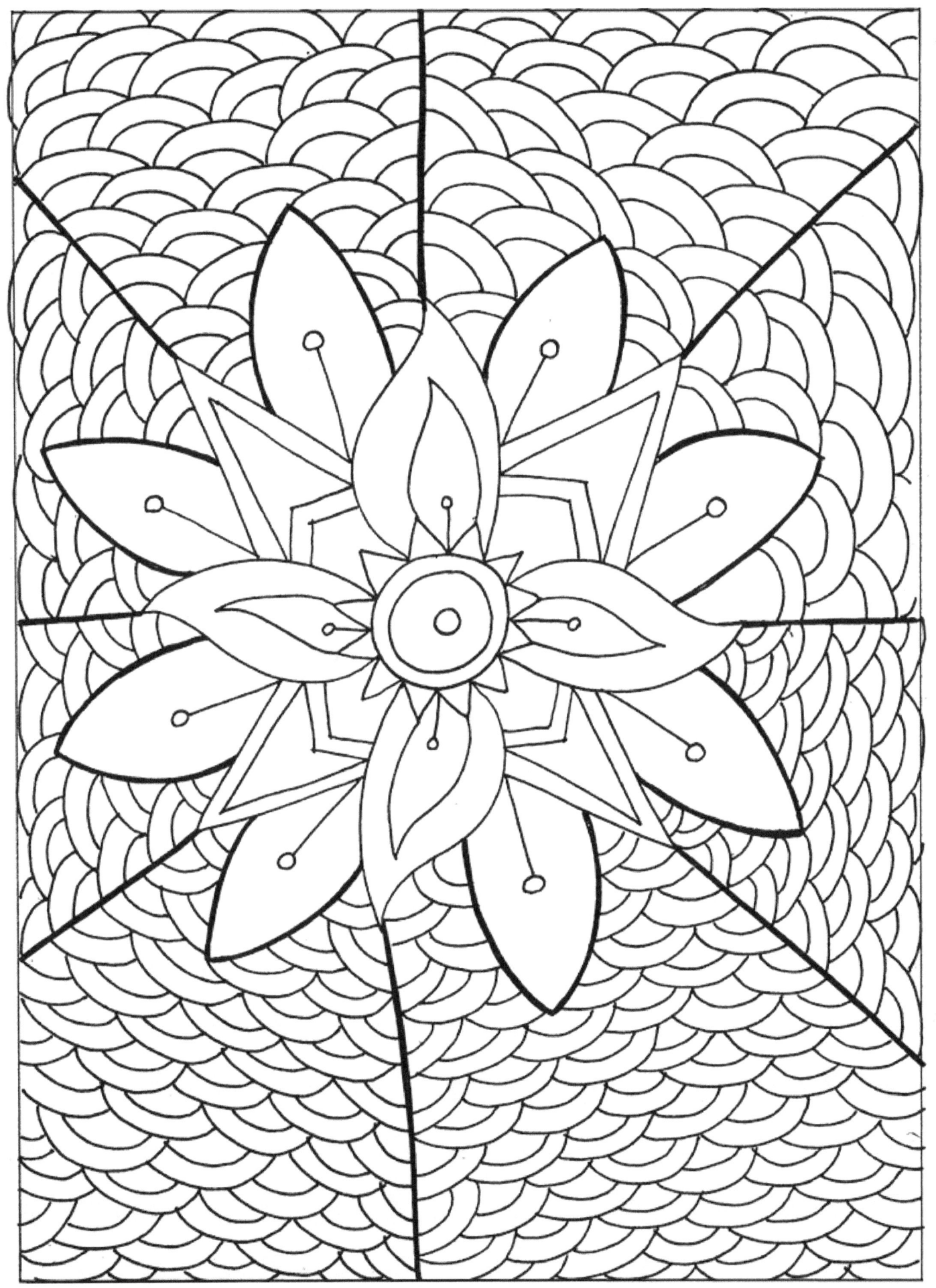

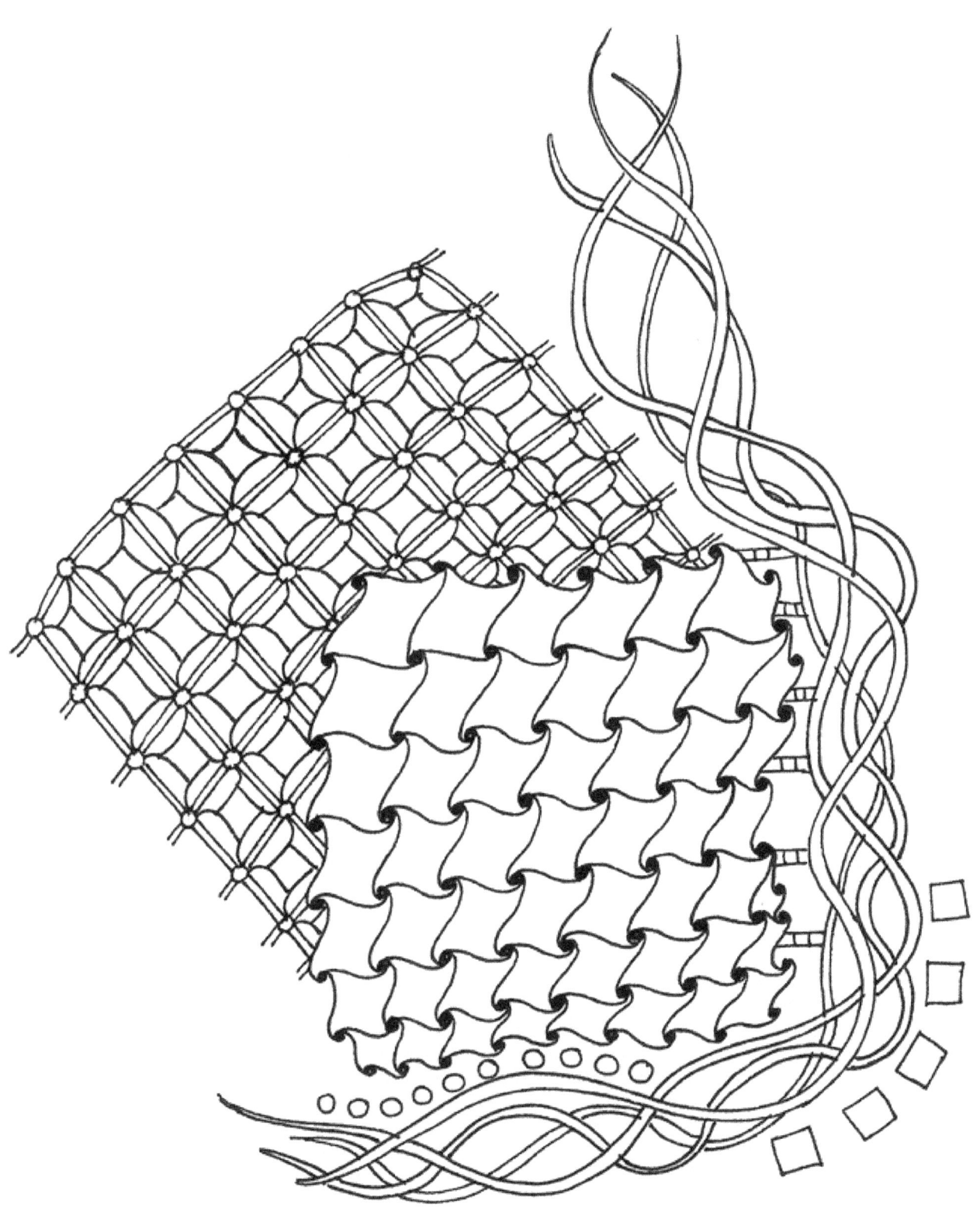

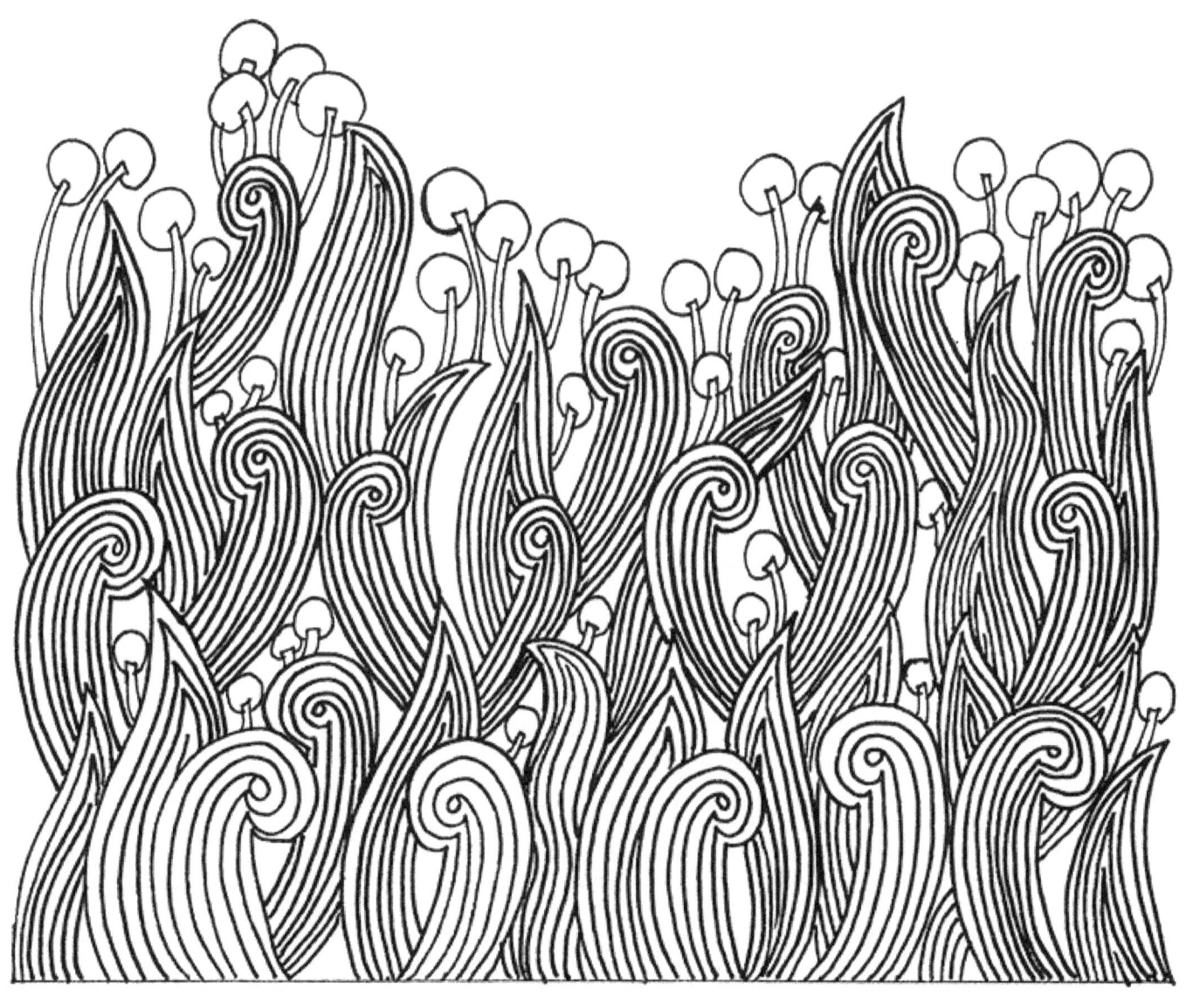

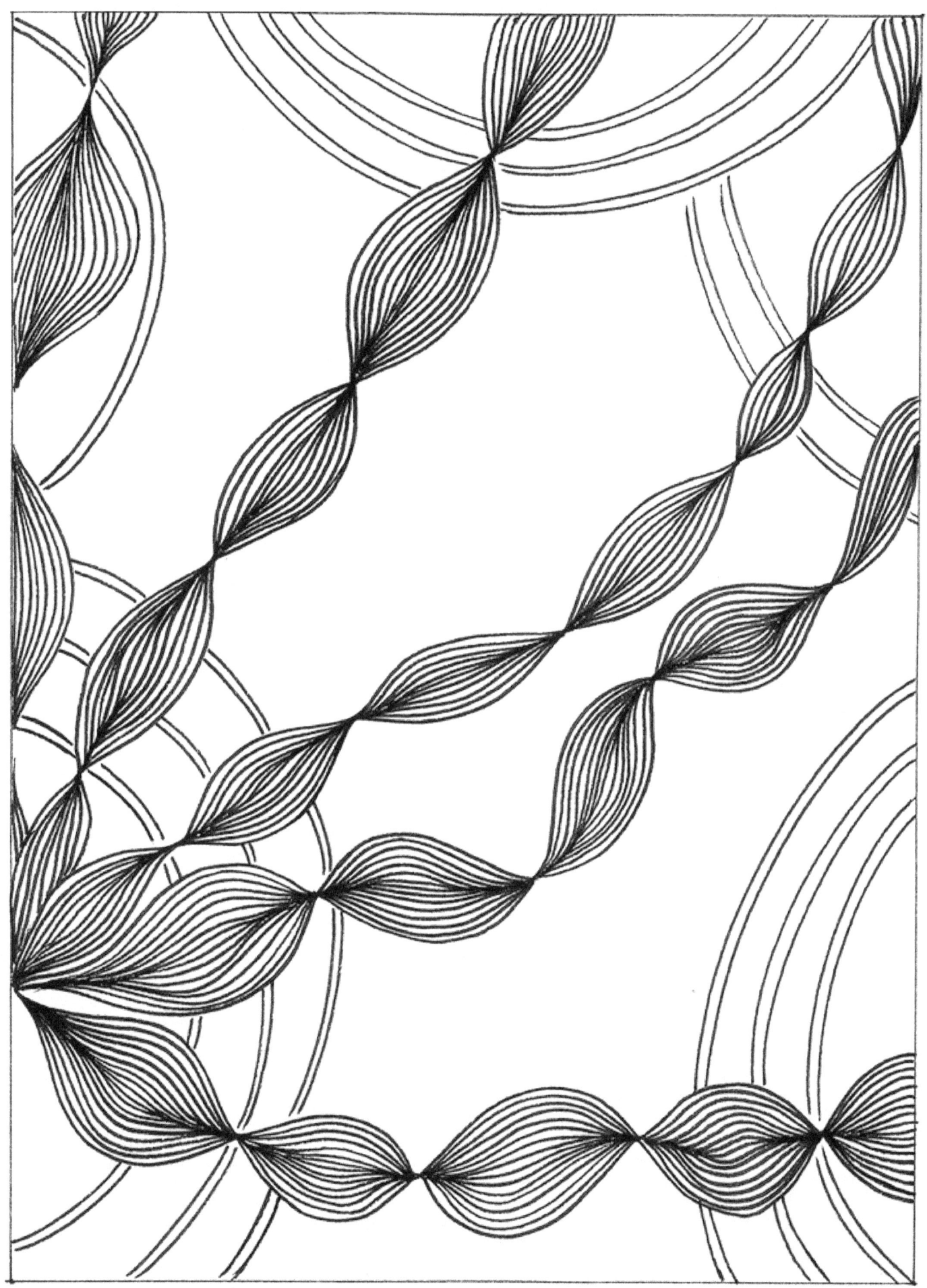

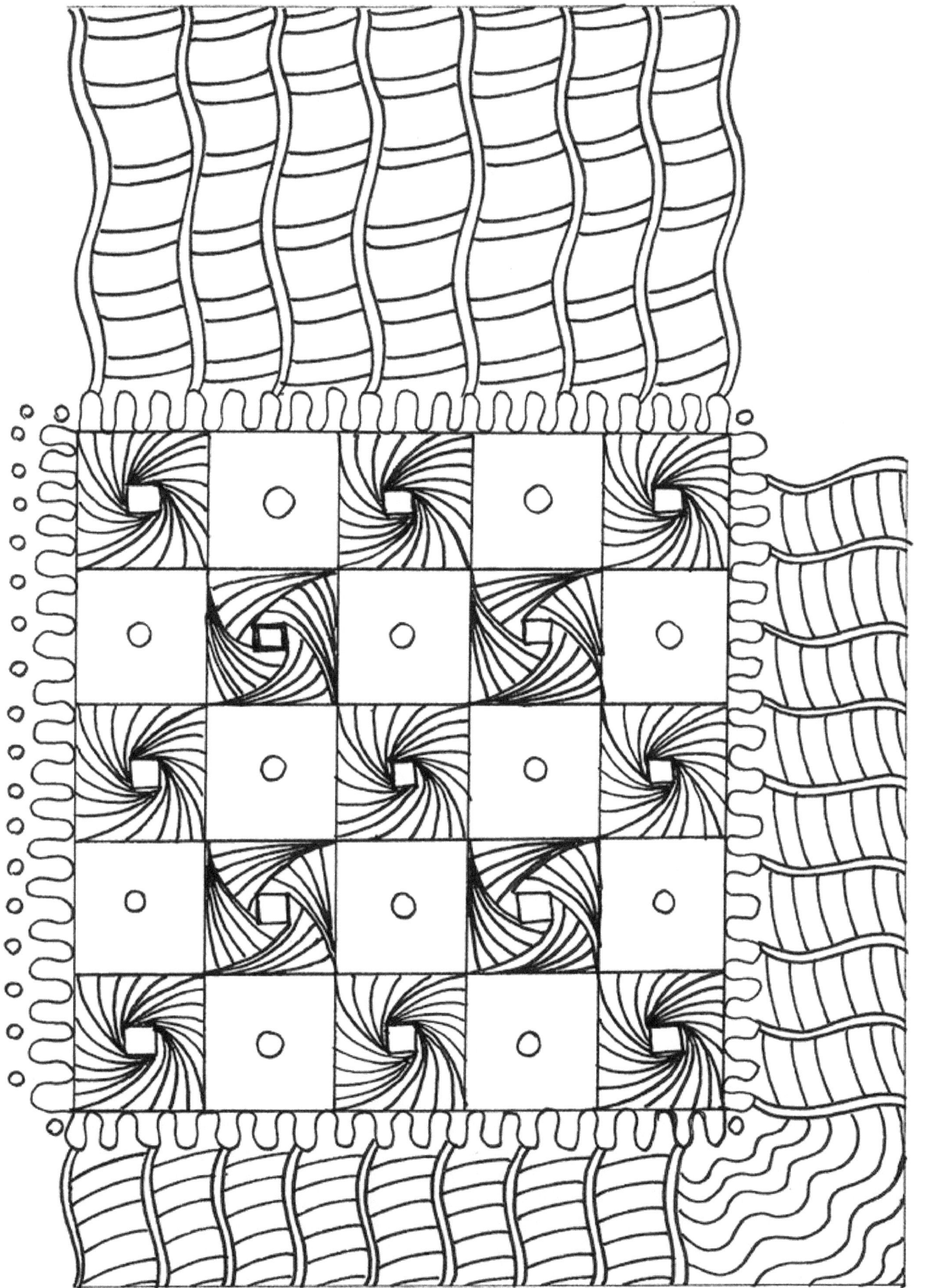

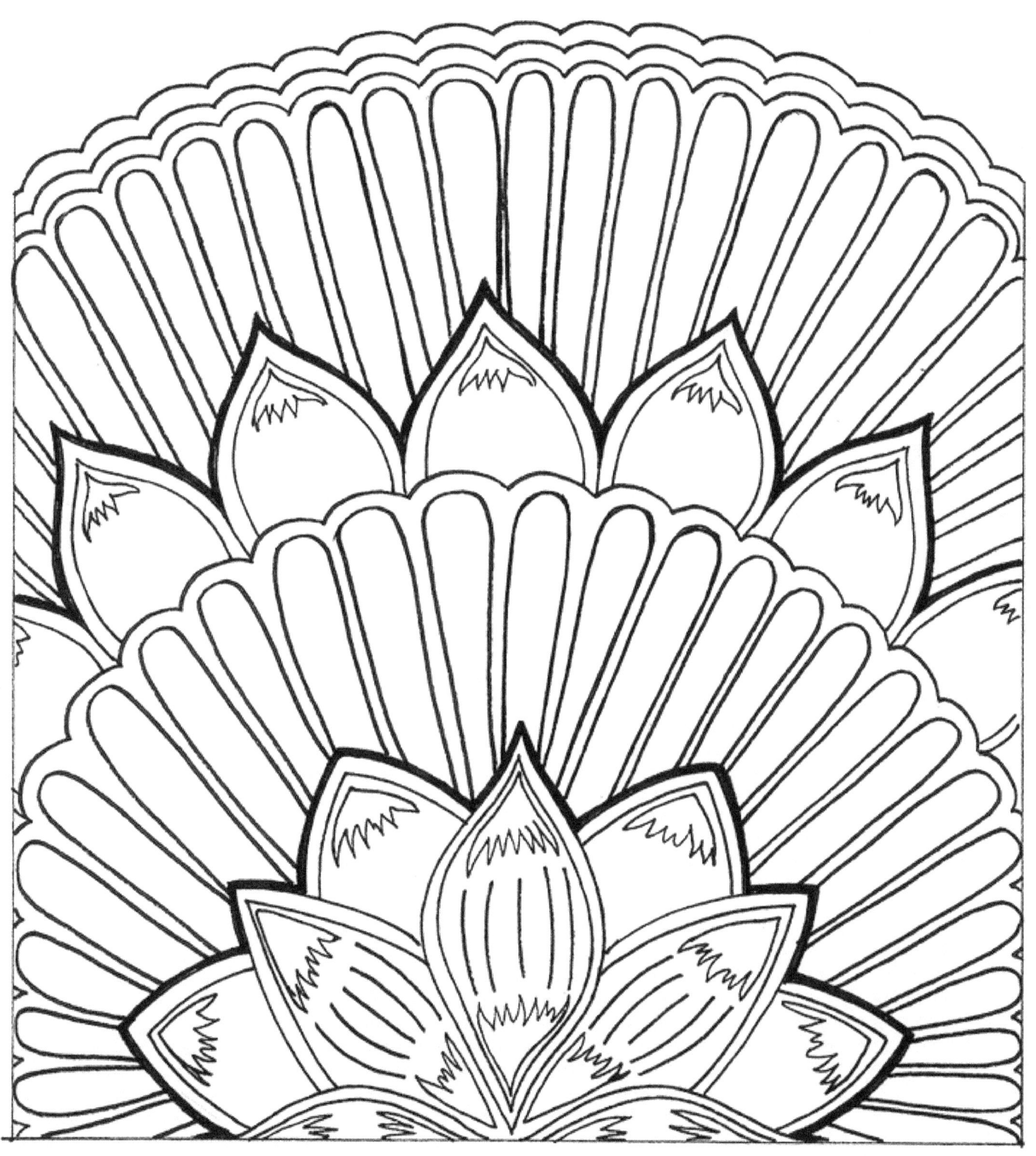

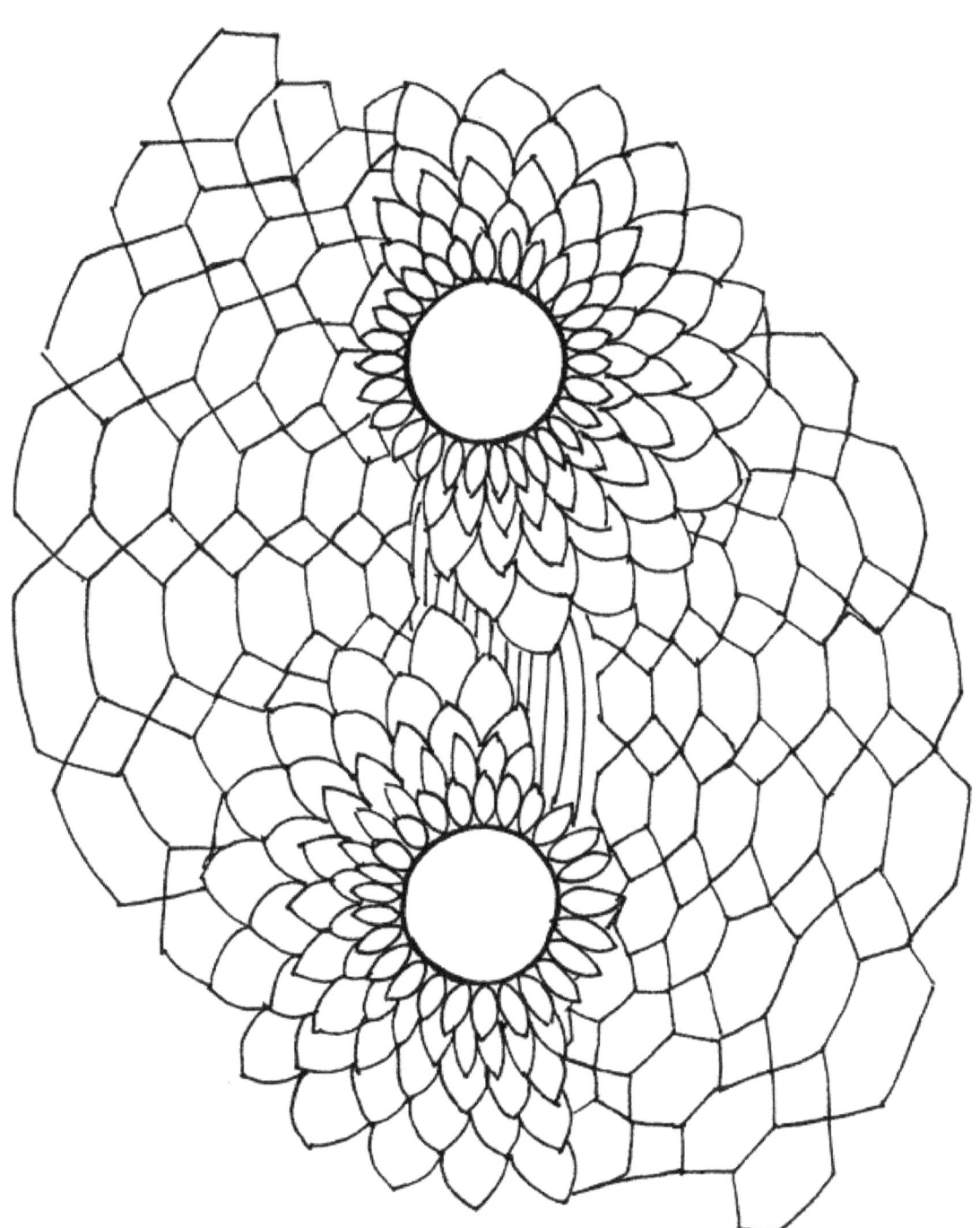

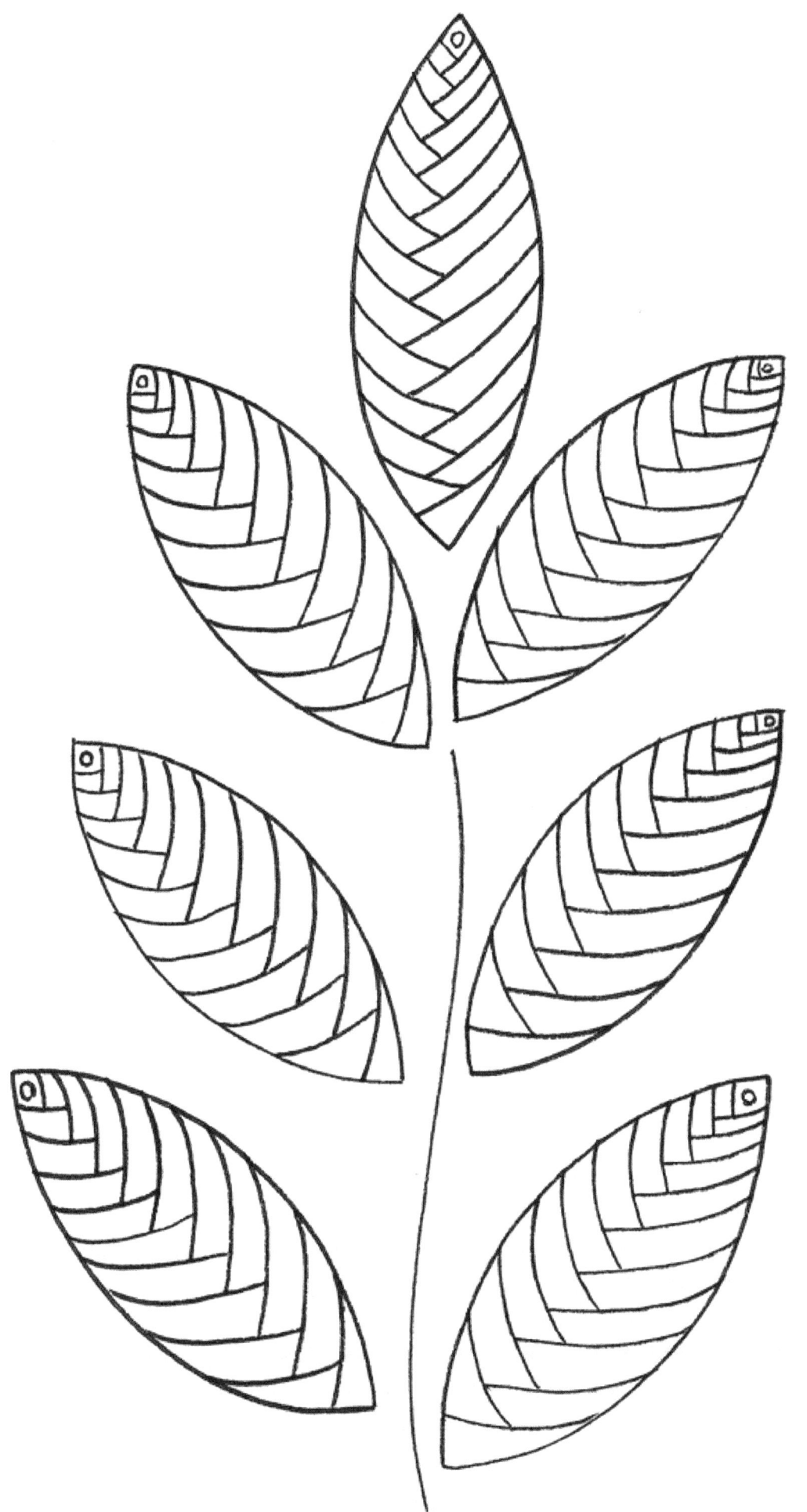

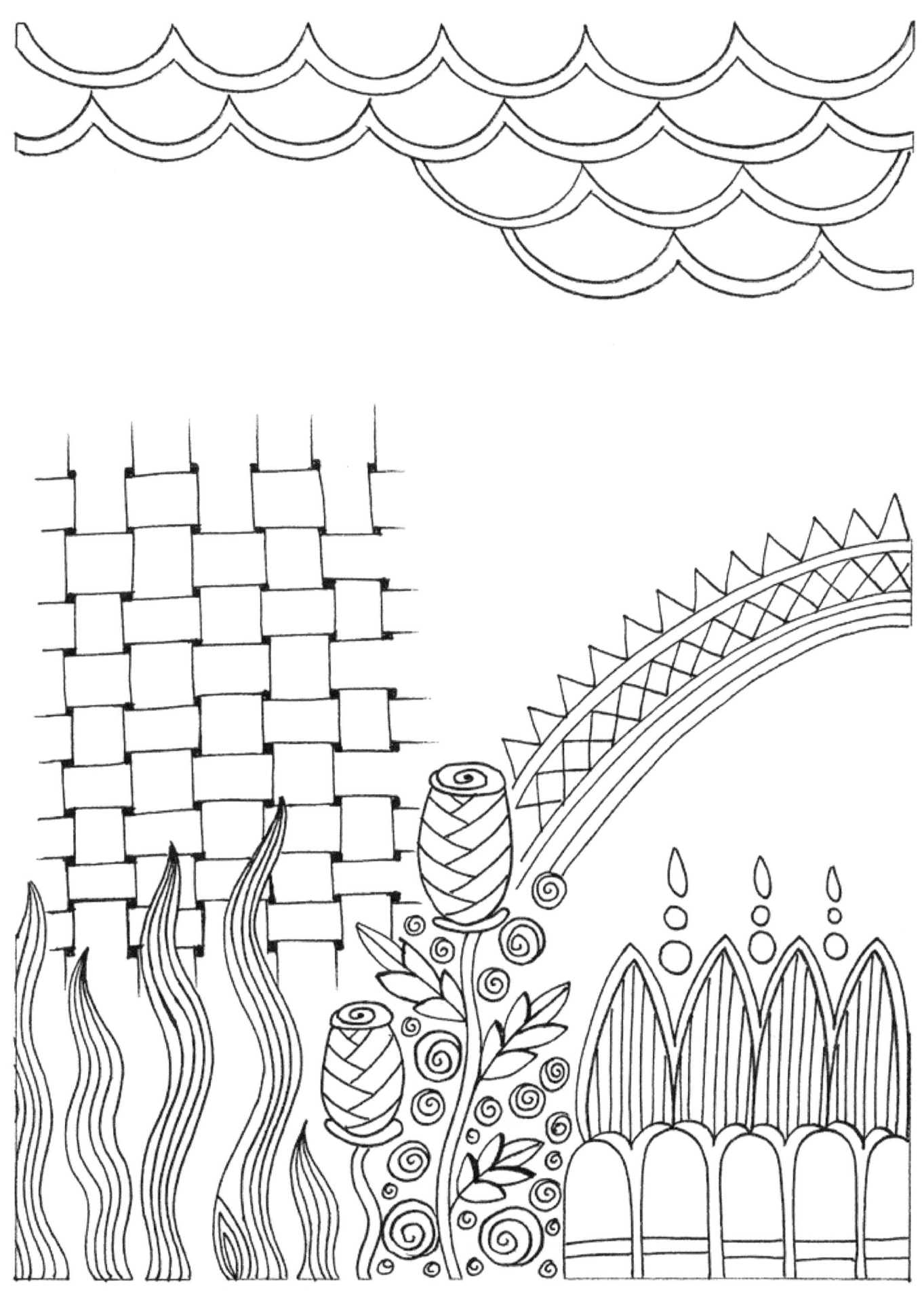

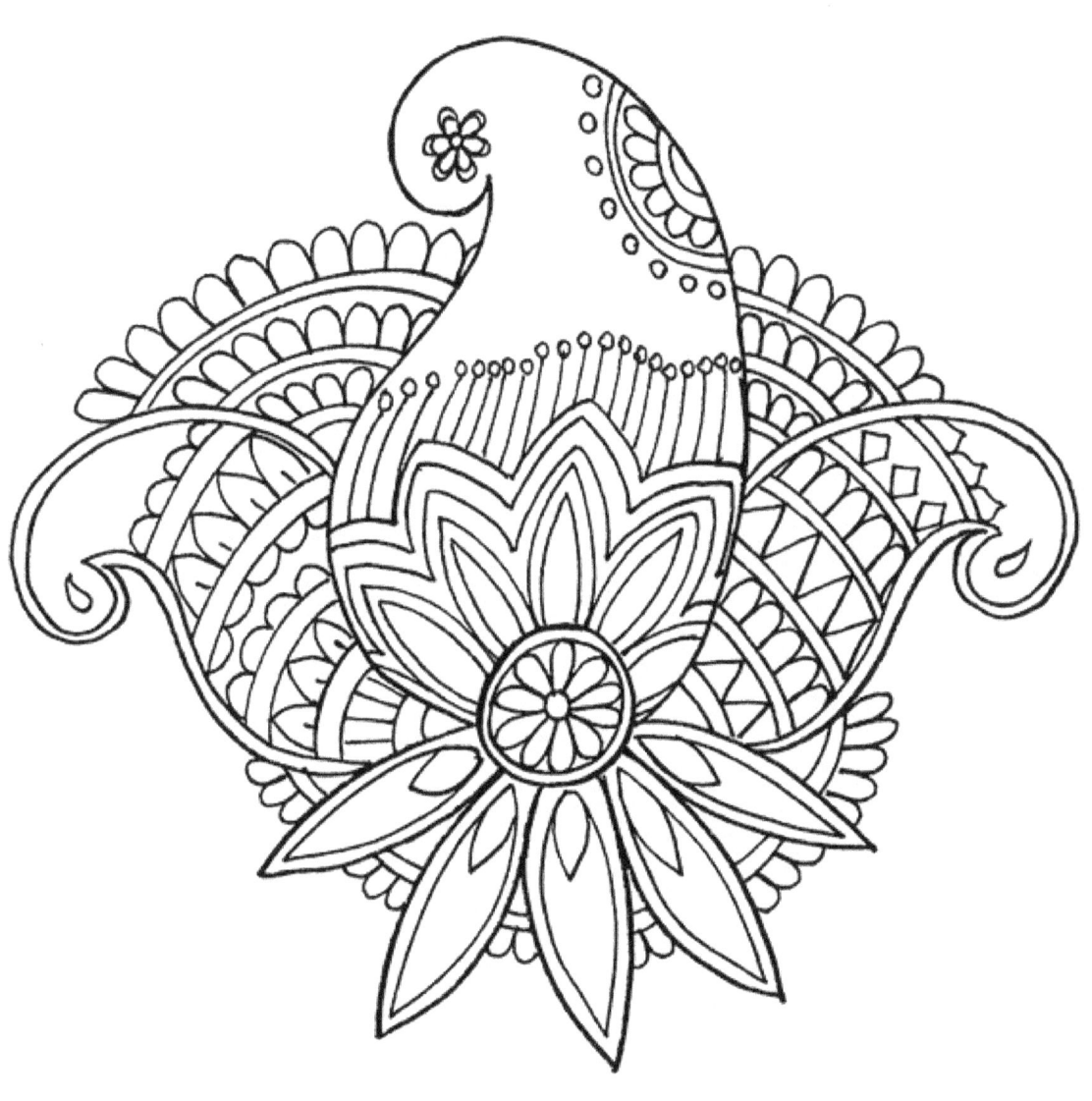

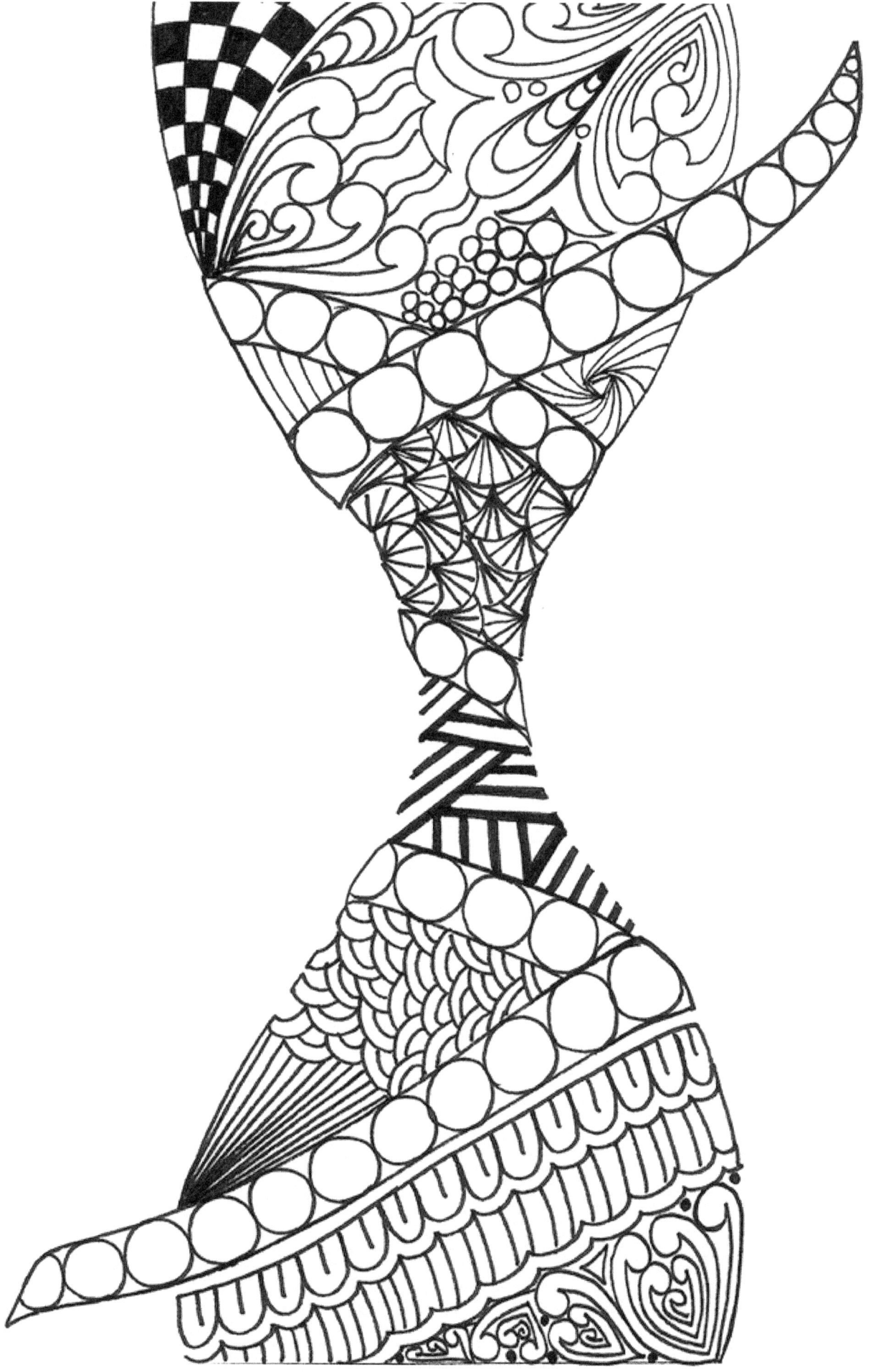

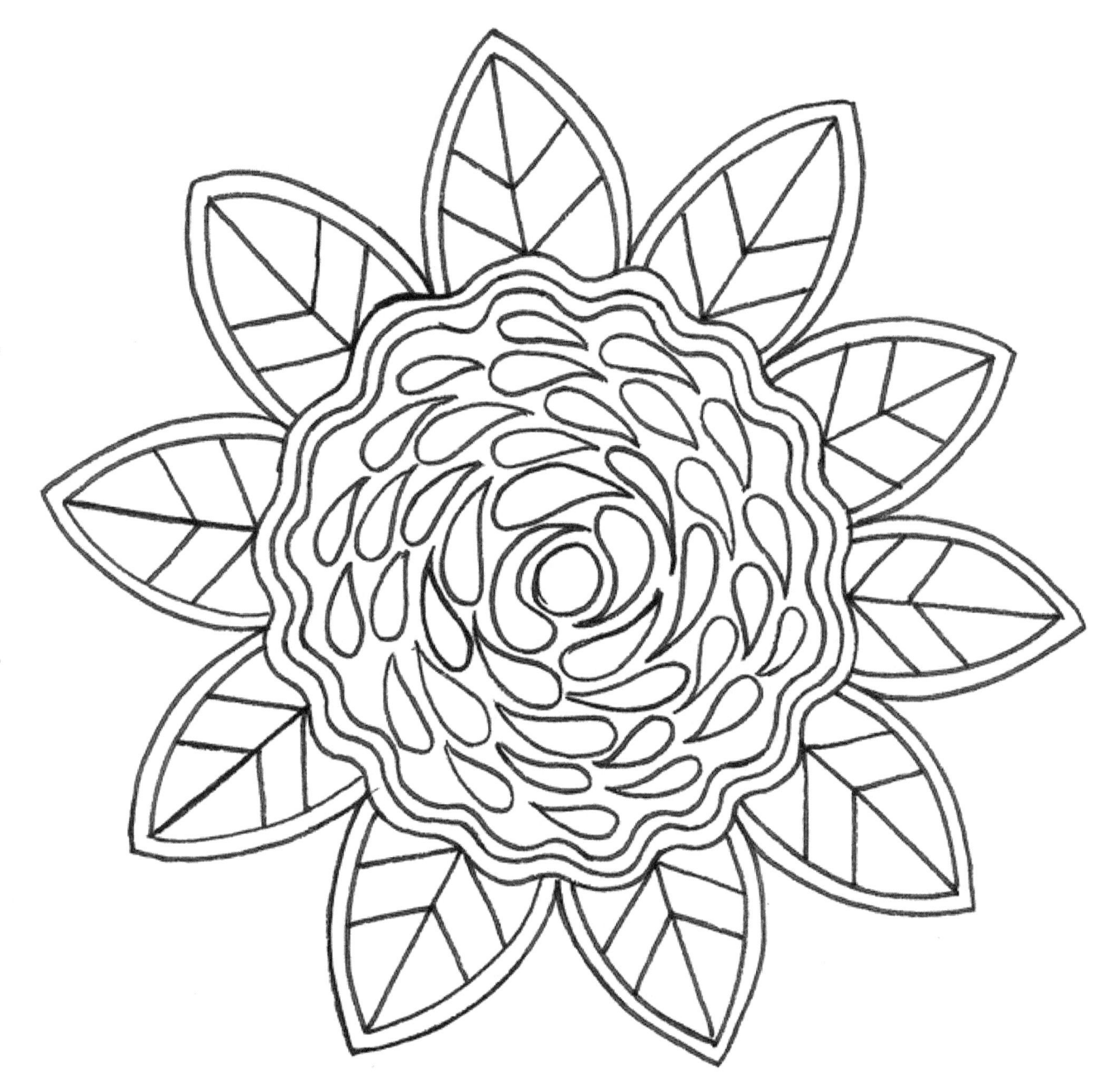